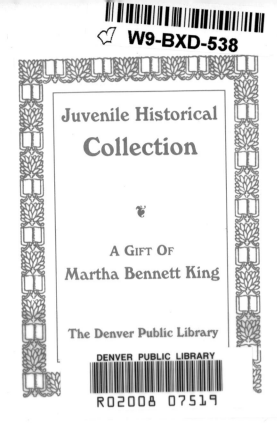

How the People
Sang the
Mountains Up

How the People Sang the Mountains Up

How and Why Stories by MARIA LEACH

Illustrated by Glen Rounds

The Viking Press   New York

Grateful acknowledgment is made to the following for permission to reprint copyrighted material:

Funk & Wagnalls, A Division of Reader's Digest Books, Inc., for "Who?" from *The Beginning: Creation Myths Around the World* by Maria Leach. Copyright 1956 by Funk & Wagnalls, N.Y.

Rutgers University Press for "Why God Made the Dog—Rumania" and "Dog's Hoop—Lipan Apache" from *God Had a Dog* by Maria Leach.

The Viking Press, Inc. and Angus & Robertson Ltd. for "How the Sun Was Made" from *Australian Legendary Tales* collected by K. Langloh Parker. All rights reserved.

First published in 1967 by The Viking Press, Inc.
625 Madison Avenue, New York, N.Y. 10022

Published simultaneously in Canada by
The Macmillan Company of Canada Limited

Library of Congress catalog card number: AC 67–10646

398   1. Folklore
       2. Animal folklore

Printed in U. S. A. by The Murray Printing Co.

Contents

Man

Animals

Questions and Answers

WHY things are as they are (did it all start with nothing?), HOW everything—the earth, the living plants and animals, and we ourselves—began to be: these questions have been important to the mind of man ever since the mind of man began to wonder.

The stories in this book are why and how stories. They come to us from all over the world, from wherever the first thinkers, the first questioners looked at the stars or the hills or the sea or listened to their own hearts beat, and stopped to say "Why?—How?"

The ancient Egyptians explained the earth and man as just "the thought that came into the heart of the god," and the god's word made the thought reality; and therefore the god dwells in every living thing and in the heart of man.

There are three kinds of why stories: the serious and mythical; the entertaining, merely amusing and anecdotal; and the legendary, explaining some local phenomenon or geographic feature.

Those which start with creation are actually origin myths or constitute an episode contained within a long explanatory creation myth. They explain the beginning of the world, the stars, the seas, the winds, the origin of animals and their brothers, man; they explain how people got the first corn or wheat or bread or bananas,

9

how they got fire or learned to make it. They explain the gift of laughter or sleep or song, the origins of games and religious ceremonies, and of old age and death. Some of these are part of every child's education within the cultures in which they are told.

Jicarilla Apache men and women, boys and girls, who learn the wonderful myth about how the people sang their own mountains into existence are allowed to part their hair on the side and paint the part red. But they must know the story without error.

Why stories that are told for entertainment sometimes border on the noodle story, like "How Turtle Keeps from Getting Wet," (p. 116). The one about the tug-of-war between Whale and Elephant is classified as a trickster tale with Rabbit, of course, in the role of trickster.

The story "How Chipmunk Got His Stripes" in this book (p. 75) is part of the story of the world, part of the serious business of establishing day and night; but there is another story about how Chipmunk got his stripes, in which Chipmunk and his grandmother were picking berries. Chipmunk said, "My back itches; scratch me." So Grandmother scratched him, and today you can still see the stripes. This brief anecdote obviously is not a serious myth but is told just for fun.

One of the most famous why stories in the world is one of Aesop's fables. It answers the question why three times. Long ago the diver-bird, the bat, and the thornbush went into partnership in the wool business. They loaded a big ship with wool to go around the world, but the ship was shipwrecked and the three partners lost everything. This is why the bat sulks all day and comes out only at night, why the diver-bird dives and dives (he is looking for the lost ship), and this is why the thornbush grabs hold of sheep or people with warm clothes. He is trying to get back his wool.

10

This, of course, is just an entertaining why story, not a solemn myth or a local legend.

The why story is also often told to explain some local landmark, such as marks on rocks (made by the culture hero), high cliffs, winding rivers, or place names, such as Adam's Peak in Ceylon, where Adam landed when hurled out of Paradise, or Devil's Ear Mountain in the Adirondacks, or the Pilot Mountains in Maine, so called for the dog named Pilot who searched the woods for his lost master, found and led him back to his mountain camp.

The magical power of song turns up in several stories in this book. We find this belief all over the world, from the ancient Icelandic Eddas to the Incas of Peru and into Africa. It is a special feature, however, of North American Indian mythology, especially in the Southwest and among North Pacific Coast tribes, but we find it also among the Iroquois of the Central Woodlands. The Iroquois singer sings for the creative power of the song; he sings for life itself.

Songs might begin with the words "I wish ——" or "I hope ——," change to "It is becoming, it is happening ——," and end with the words that such and such a thing *has become, has happened*—like Chipmunk's song for daylight (p. 75) which ends with the words "Light will come," and like Rabbit's song in "How Rabbit Stole Fire from the Buzzards," which ends with the words "Now the people will be warm." Singing that such and such is happening or true makes it happen, makes it true.

EARTH, SKY, AND SEA

Allá está la luna
Comiendo su tuna
Y echando las cáscaras
  En la laguna.

There hangs the moon
Eating her orange
And throwing the peeling
Into the lake.
                    —Mexico

Who?

In the beginning there was only water. And Someone said, "Who will make the land?"

"I will make the land," said Crawfish. And he dived down to the bottom of that great sea and stirred up the mud with his eight legs and his tail. And he took the mud in his fingers and made a little pile.

The owners of the mud down there said, "Who is stirring up the mud?" And they watched to see. But Crawfish kept stirring up the mud with his tail so they could not see.

Every day Crawfish dived into the deep water and got a little more mud and put it on the pile. Day by day he piled it up. At last one day as he piled the mud on top of the pile, his hands came out of the water into the air! The land appeared above the water.

It was very soft, for it was mud.

Someone said, "Who will stretch out the land? Who will make it hard? Who will make it dry?"

Buzzard stretched out the earth and dried it. He spread his long wings and stretched it. He sailed over the earth; he spread it wide and dried it. Then, tiring, he had to flap his wings and this made the mountains and valleys.

Someone said, "Who will make the light?"

Star said, "I will make light." But it was not enough.

It was said, "Who will make more light?"

"I will make light," said Moon. But it was still night.

Someone said, "More light."

Sun said, "I will make light. I am the mother."

So Sun moved over into the east, and all at once a great beautiful light spread over the world. And then as Sun moved from east to west, a drop of her blood fell and sank into the earth. From this blood and this earth came forth the first people, the Yuchi Indians. They called themselves Tsohaya, People of the Sun, and every man who took this name had a picture of the sun on his door.

—*Yuchi-Creek*

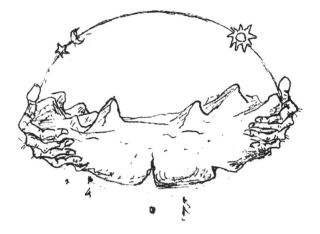

How the Earth
Was Made To Fit the Sky

Long before the earth was made, long before there was a sky, there was Zongma, the greatest, greatest god. He had two sons: Nipu and Nili, two unknown ones in the nothingness.

Ages went by. Then one day Nili made the earth and Nipu made the sky.

The earth was too big. When Nipu made the sky and laid it like a lid over the earth, the earth was too big. The lid did not fit.

"Make the earth smaller, Brother," said Nipu, "so that the sky will fit."

So Nili squeezed and pinched up the mud until great ridges and peaks of it rose into the air and stood there—high.

Then Nipu laid the sky over the earth once more, and it fit.

That is the way it is today: the sky bends over the earth and touches the rim of the world; and the mountains rise up and stand in their places.

—Bugun

How the Sun Was Made

There was no sun at first. For a long time there were only moon and stars. There were no men, only birds and animals.

One day Dinewan, the emu, and Brolga, the crane, were quarreling. Brolga was so mad that she rushed to Dinewan's nest, seized one of the big emu eggs, and threw it with all her strength up into the sky.

It landed on a heap of firewood up there; the yellow yolk spilled out of it, and the firewood burst into flame. The blaze was so bright that it lighted up the whole world.

The sky spirit who lived in the sky looked down and saw the earth illumined and bright and beautiful in the light.

Good! he thought. Good! There should be a fire every day. And he has made the fire faithfully every day from that time to this.

He sends the morning star out first to let the world know that the fire will soon blaze up. But so many people sleep and never see the star that he thought there ought to be some kind of noise to waken heavy sleepers.

All the sky spirits consulted together trying to decide who should be the one to wake up the world. Then one day they heard the laughing jackass laugh.

"That is the right noise," they said. (The laughing jackass is the big Australian kingfisher, about the size of a crow, whose loud cry sounds like a laugh.)

So they told the laughing jackass to laugh loud every morning so the people would know that the sun was rising.

He does. Laughing jackass saves the light of the world every day in Australia. He knows that if he did not laugh at sunrise, there would be no sun, and darkness would take the world again forever.

—Euahlayi

Why Sun and Moon
Live in the Sky

Long ago Sun lived on the earth and was good friends with Water. Every day Sun went to see Water, but Water never visited Sun. This did not lessen the friendship, however. Sun kept right on going to see Water.

One day Sun said, "Water, why do you never come to my house? Why don't you come to see me?"

"Your house is not big enough," said Water. "If I came I would push you out."

Sun wanted Water to visit him anyway. He kept asking him to come. So finally Water said, "All right, but you must build a big place. You must build a tremendous place, because my people have to come with me."

Sun said he would do that and went home to tell Moon, his wife.

The next day he began to build. He built a great big enormous enclosure, so big he was sure it would hold Water.

When it was finished Sun went to tell Water.

"Come," he said. "The big place is finished. Come for a visit."

So Water started out. As he approached the place he called out, "Is it all right? Is it safe if I come in?"

"Yes, my dear friend. Come in! Come in!" cried Sun joyfully.

Water began to flow into the place and some fish came along with him.

Pretty soon the water was knee-deep.

"Is it safe?" said Water. "Shall I come in?"

"Yes," said Sun. "Come in."

So Water flowed in. Some more fish came along too and a lot of water animals.

By this time the water was neck-high.

"Shall I keep coming?" said Water.

"Oh, yes," said Sun and Moon together, "do."

So in poured Water until Sun and Moon had to sit on the roof of their house.

"Am I pushing you out?" said Water. "Shall I come in?"

"Oh, yes," said Sun and Moon.

On came the rushing water, with more fish and more sea animals. And when the roof was covered, Sun and Moon flew into the sky.

And there they are.

—*Efik*

How the Earth's
Fire Was Saved

Long ago the old gods sent the waters to rise up and cover the earth. So the waters swelled and advanced upon the land.

Fire was afraid. Fire ran ahead of the water. Fire ran and ran, and the water flowed and followed. Finally there was no place to go. The coming waters were surely going to put Fire out forever.

Then Fire saw a little piece of iron in the ground, so he hid in that. It was not big enough, so he went into the rocks and stones—deep down into the heart of rock and stone. But there were not enough stones.

Fire saw two tall bamboo trees ahead. He leaped up and hid inside the bamboo trees.

Everybody knows today, of course, that there is fire hidden in the trees and in the rocks. There are some stories in this book about how mankind learned to let it out.

—Tinguian

How the People Sang
the Mountains Up

Silence. Dark. There was nothing there. Only the Hactcins, the Holy Ones, were there from the beginning. They owned the stuff of creation. There was no light—just darkness and the Hactcins creating things in the dark.

Black Hactcin was the great creator. He made all the animals and told them to walk, and they walked. He told the birds how to fly, and they flew. Hactcin created a man and told him to speak and to walk and to laugh. Then he made a woman. After that the people were many.

It was dark down there where the people lived because there was no sun. So Black Hactcin called for White Hactcin to come, because White Hactcin owned the sun stuff.

"The people need light," said Black Hactcin.

White Hactcin looked in his bag and took out a little sun.

"This will make daylight," he said.

Then Black Hactcin looked in his bag and took out a little moon.

"This can shine in the night," he said.

The sun and the moon were very small and dim.

"You had better start singing," said Black Hactcin.

So they sang together to make the sun and moon grow larger; and as they sang, the sun and moon began to grow; their light became strong and bright; and the sun and moon moved in their courses, just as they do today.

But it was still dim where the people were. The sun and moon were too far away, too high. What the people needed was a mountain.

Then the Hactcins made four little mounds of earth for the people. In each one they hid the seeds and fruits which were to grow, and on top of each little mound they laid the leaves and needles of the trees which were to grow on the mountain.

The little mounds stood in a row, east to west. One was a little mound of black earth, one was of blue earth, one was yellow earth, and the fourth was glittering earth. All mountains are made of these four kinds of earth. Then the Hactcins filled a black clay bowl with water (because nothing can grow without water) and they watered the little mounds.

All the animals and birds and people were there and helped to make the mounds grow. They all sang and the mountain began to rise. They were all using their power.

They sang and sang, and the mountain grew and the fruits and trees began to grow on the mountain. They sang four times and the mountain grew, twelve times and the mountain grew twelve times. As it grew, the four little mounds merged together and grew into one big mountain. This spread into a long, beautiful range.

Then the people began traveling up the mountains. The birds flew up first, then came the animals and the people. They climbed and climbed and finally came forth into a sunny world.

When the people were all up the mountains in the sun, the Hactcins put a white pot upside down on top of the highest peak, so all would remember it forever. Some say it rises north of Durango, Colorado, one of the peaks of the San Juan Mountains.

—*Jicarilla Apache*

24

Why the Tides Ebb and Flow

1.

This happened long ago when the people were learning how to live in the world. The people had no food. They were starving.

One day when Raven was out on the ocean in his canoe, following along the shores and beaches, he saw fish swimming under the water. He saw crabs crawling, mussels lying in their beds, little clams sticking their necks out. Starfish rambled around on their strange circular advance.

"The people could eat these things if they could get them," said Raven.

Raven, culture hero of all Northwest Pacific Coast peoples, was fixing up the world and teaching people how to live. He thought all people should have enough to eat. He was the one who fixed the earth so it would not tip. He put a big piece of ice across the north of it, and since then it has not tipped. Raven fixed the world and taught the people everything.

The people could eat these things if they could get them, he kept thinking, but the water is too deep.

25

Raven paddled along, paddled along, wondering what to do. Then he saw a great big man sitting on the shore.

"What are you doing there?" said Raven.

"Sitting," said the man.

"Why?"

"If I get up the ocean will go dry," said the man. "So I sit."

The man was sitting on a hole in the earth. If he got up, the ocean poured into the hole.

"Get up and let me look," said Raven.

"No," said the man. He would not budge.

So Raven grabbed him by the hair and pulled him up. Sure enough, there was a bottomless hole in the earth, and when the man stood up, the ocean waters poured and roared into it.

Raven slid a sharp stone alongside the hole with his foot. When the man sat down, the stone jabbed him and he jumped up. Raven

slipped another sharp-pointed stone under him, so that when the man sat, this hurt worse, and the man leaped into the air again.

While this was going on, the waters poured into the hole; the ocean receded, and the beach was uncovered.

Yes. The people can get food here, Raven decided.

"From now on," said Raven to the man, "you must stand up twice every day, long enough to let the waters recede as far as they are now, so that the people may find food."

"All right," said the man. "All right."

Thus it is that the tides began to ebb and flow and people gathered seafood on the shores.

—Tahltan

2.

There is a great big hole in the bottom of the ocean, and in it lives a monstrous giant crab.

Twice every day the crab comes forth to look for food. He crawls around on the bottom of the ocean and on the sandy beaches of the world to see what he can find.

While he is doing this, the waters of the ocean pour into the hole, and the rivers that flow into the seas pour into the hole. Then it is low tide along the shores.

When the giant crab goes home again and backs into his hole, he takes up all the space there is. The waters of the seas gush and gurgle and pour out of the hole around him. As he settles in, they rise and the waves roll toward the land and break against the shores. That is high tide.

—Malay

Why the Sea Is Salt

A long time ago Frodi, son of Fridleif, was king of Denmark. He was called Peace Frodi, the greatest of the Northland kings.

One time he went to visit Fjölnir, king of Sweden, and there he bought two big maidservants, "huge and strong," named Fenja and Menja. When he saw them, he thought, They can grind the mill; for Frodi had a big mill named Grótti back in Denmark. It had two millstones so big that no one could lift or turn them. These were magic millstones which would grind forth whatever the turner asked for.

So Frodi brought Fenja and Menja to the mill and told them to grind forth gold. This they did willingly. They sang for gold, and gold and peace and prosperity piled up for Frodi. Frodi, however, at the sight of gold became greedy. He wanted more and more and forgot to give the girls rest or time to sleep.

When finally they had worked beyond their strength and Frodi still cried "More!" Fenja and Menja changed their song. They sang for sleep and ground forth sleep until Frodi and all his warriors slept. Then they sang for vengeance, and the mill began to grind forth hosts of men who rose up and killed Frodi and his people.

Mysingr, the sea king, took the ship. He stole all the gold, and the mill, and the two big maidservants also.

Mysingr, too, put the big handsome girls to work. They were the only ones who could turn the millstones, and he bade them grind out salt.

So Fenja and Menja ground salt from the mill now in Mysingr's ship. At night they said, "Are you not weary of salt, Mysingr?"

"More salt," said Mysingr.

So they ground more salt. The salt piled up. That very night there was so much salt that the ship sank with the weight of it, and all the salt sank into the sea. The sea has been salt from that day to this.

Only Fenja and Menja knew how to stop the mill, so it is grinding down there yet perhaps. Men have been trying through the centuries to separate salt from sea water; but the sea is still salt.

There is a great whirlpool in the sea where the millstones sank down. The waters pour down through the hole in the millstones and are whirled up again boiling white. This is the famous and terrible Maelstrom in the Norwegian Sea northwest of Norway.

—Old Norse

Who the Man in the Moon Is

1. THE OLD MAN AND HIS BUSH

The Tatars of Altai in Siberia say there is an old man in the moon who used to live on earth and eat people.

Sun said, "I'll stop that. I'll go get him and bring him into the sky."

He started out but when he got halfway to earth, he discovered that his heat was going to burn up the world and all the people.

"Never mind. I'll go," said Moon. So Moon went.

He soon found the old man standing by a hawthorn bush picking haws. Moon grabbed him up, and the old man hung on to the bush. That didn't bother Moon. He just pulled a little and sailed off with the old man still trailing his bush behind him.

You can still see the old man picking haws off the bush across the moon's face.

2. THE OLD HUMPBACK

In the Malay Peninsula the spots on the moon are said to represent an old, old humpbacked man sitting under a banana tree. He is plaiting a fishing line out of strands of banana-tree bark.

When the fishing line is finished, he is going to fish up everything on earth and have everything for himself. This has never happened yet, however, even though the old man has been at it since the beginning of time.

It has never happened so far, that is, because every night a rat gnaws through the line and saves us. The old man has to begin all over again every morning.

This is a smart rat. The old man has a smart cat, too, who is always watching for the rat and trying to catch it.

If the old man ever finishes the job, if he ever finishes braiding the fishing line, and if the line ever reaches the earth, that will be the end of the world.

3. FROGS IN THE MOON

The Lillooet Indians of British Columbia tell a story about three frog sisters who lived in a swamp. Snake and Beaver lived nearby. They wanted to marry the Frog Girls.

One night Snake went into their house and crawled into bed with one of them. He put his hand on her face to wake her.

"Who's that?" she said.

"Me. I'm Snake."

"Go away, small eyes," said Frog Girl. So Snake went away. His feelings were hurt. He told Beaver.

31

The next night Beaver went to the Frog Girls' house. He crawled into bed with one of them and put his hand on her face to wake her.

"Who's that?" she said.

"Me. I'm Beaver."

"Go away, short legs," said Frog Girl. So Beaver went away. His feelings were hurt and he began to cry.

"What's the matter?" said the old beaver father. Beaver told him what Frog Girl had said and cried some more.

"Never mind," said the old beaver. "Stop crying or it will rain too much."

But young Beaver went right on crying, and after a while it started to rain. (Everyone knows that the beaver's cry brings rain.) It rained and rained.

Soon the swamp was flooded and the Frog Girls' house was under water. The Frog Girls were wet and cold.

They went to Beaver's house and asked to come in.

"No," said the old beaver father. "You called our boys bad names."

So the Frog Girls swam away down the river until they were caught in a whirlpool and whirled right into Moon's house.

Moon was sorry for them. "Come in and get warm by the fire," said Moon.

"No, we'll sit HERE," they said and jumped right into the moon's face.

The Frog Girls are still there. You can see them.

4. HJUKI AND BIL

In the old time when the moon was new, the moon's name was Mani. So says the Old Norse myth in Snorri Sturluson's *Prose Edda*.

One day Mani saw two children drawing water from a well. They had a long pole across their shoulders and a bucket or cask hung from the pole. The boy's name was Hjuki and the girl was called Bil. They were the children of a man named Vithfinner, who made them work too hard.

Mani was sorry for them; he stole the children and took them off to his house on the moon. They can still be seen today, with bucket and pole, on the full moon's face. As the moon wanes, they fall out of sight; first Hjuki, then Bil goes "tumbling after." As the moon waxes, they take up pole and bucket again "to fetch a pail of water."

Children have heard this story in other words for about 150 years:

Jack and Jill went up the hill
To fetch a pail of water.

33

Jack fell down and broke his crown
And Jill came tumbling after.

We do not know for sure that our Jack and Jill rhyme comes from this story; but it is a charming explanation.

5. THE MOON'S FACE

The Masai people of Kenya in East Africa have an old myth which says that Sun and Moon were man and wife. Shortly after they were married they had a big fight and beat each other up. Each one damaged the other.

After it was all over Sun was very much ashamed—so ashamed that he blazed into so bright a brightness that now nobody can look at him.

Moon was not ashamed, however. Moon did not care. She just sails across the sky and does not care who sees that her mouth is swollen and crooked and that she has only one eye.

MAN

How the People Began

Long, long ago, soon after the earth fell out of the sky and became the earth, men rose up. They rose up out of the earth from under the willow trees, brushed off the willow leaves that stuck to them, and walked about.

Nobody today remembers those first astonishing days; but there were men and women there, walking about. It is known that the women found children somewhere and sewed clothes for them, and the children grew up to be men and women. Thus there were people in the world.

The men wanted dogs. They needed dogs. So one man made a dog leash and went out to call the dogs' call.

He called "Hok!—hok!" and the dogs came running. They rose up out of the sand dunes and hummocks and came running to man, shaking the sand from their coats.

The days went by and the people lived their lives. New babies were born, and the people became many. The old ones wished to rest, but they did not know how to lie down and take the long rest that each man deserves after a long life. They did not know how to die.

There was no sun yet in the world. The people had only the light of their lamps in the houses.

One old, old woman said, "We have no light and no death."

Another old, old woman said, "Oh, I wish we could have light and death . . . "—and the wish came true. Suddenly there was light and with it came death.

After this the sun and moon and stars were in the sky. One gave light by day; one gave light by night; and every time someone died, there was a new star shining in the sky.

—Greenland Eskimo

Chameleon Finds —

At first there were no people. Only Mulungu and the decent peaceful beasts were in the world.

One day Chameleon sat weaving a fish-trap, and when he had finished he set it in the river. In the morning he pulled the trap and it was full of fish, which he took home and ate.

He set the trap again. In the morning he pulled it out and it was empty: no fish.

"Bad luck," he said and set the trap again.

The next morning when he pulled the trap he found a little man and woman in it. He had never seen any creatures like this.

"What can they be?" he said. "Today I behold the unknown." And he picked up the fish-trap and took the two creatures to Mulungu.

"Father," said Chameleon, "see what I have brought."

Mulungu looked. "Take them out of the trap," he said. "Put them down on the earth and they will grow."

Chameleon did this. And the man and woman grew. They grew until they became as tall as men and women are today.

All the animals watched to see what the people would do. They made fire. They rubbed two sticks together in a special way and thus made fire. The fire caught in the bush and roared through the forest and the animals had to run to escape the flames.

The people caught a buffalo and killed it and roasted it in the fire and ate it. Then next day they did the same thing. Every day they set fires and killed some animal and ate it.

"They are burning up everything!" said Mulungu. "They are killing my people!"

All the beasts ran into the forest as far away from mankind as they could get. Chameleon went into the high trees.

"I'm leaving!" said Mulungu.

He called to Spider. "How do you climb on high?" he said.

"Very nicely," said Spider. And Spider spun a rope for Mulungu and Mulungu climbed the rope and went to live in the sky.

Thus the gods were driven off the face of the earth by the cruelty of man.

—*Yao*

40

Creator Makes—

Long ago everything was dark. Creator sat there and thought about making sunshine. So he created Raven and said to Raven, "Go peck and peck and set free the sunrise."

Raven flew into the east and pecked, but he could not peck through to sunrise, so he gave up and went back.

Then Creator sent Wagtail. Wagtail flew into the east and pecked and pecked until he wore out his beak. At last he made one tiny hole. So he flew back to Creator and told him.

"Try again," said Creator.

Wagtail went back again and pecked and pecked until the hole grew big. The sun flashed through. There was the sunrise. There was the world's light.

Wagtail had worn out his beak and his wings. He had to walk home to Creator. There was no food along the way. When he got there, he was nothing but a skinny, little, miserable bird.

"Light flows over the earth," he said.

Creator gave Wagtail new feathers and new wings and a new sharp beak and a new nest under a grass hummock.

"Live here," said Creator. "Your food shall be the worms in the ground."

Then Creator went himself and walked around in the world. He scattered bones all over and said, "Become human beings. Live and be men."

After a while he wondered what was happening, how the world was getting along. Who shall I send for news? he thought.

"Go visit earth and mankind," he said to Ptarmigan. Ptarmigan started out but soon came back.

"Too far," he said.

Then Creator sent Polar Owl, who went and saw men but brought no news. Creator sent Yellow Fox, who started out but never got there. He sent Arctic Fox, who saw men and was afraid of them. He too came back.

Then Creator created Wolf. "Go to the earth," he said, "and bring me news of the people there."

Wolf went and looked. He saw men standing around. Wolf ran back to Creator.

"I saw men," he said. "They have eyes and eyebrows and hair on their heads. They stand up and are afraid to sit down. They are awful!"

So Creator went himself to see. He saw a man. "Sit down!" he said. The man sat. "Sit down," he said to the woman, and she sat down beside the man.

Then Creator made reindeer. "These are for you," he said to the people. The reindeer increased; fawns were born. "Reindeer skin can be your clothing," said Creator. To the people by the sea he said, "Sealskin can be your clothing."

Then Creator made a fire drill of pine wood and gave it to the man and woman so they could make fire and cook their food. (A fire drill is the most ancient fire maker mankind knew. To work it one holds a slender stick between the hands and revolves it rap-

42

idly in a slot in a small block of softer wood. The friction creates heat and fire.)

Later the people moved to a new place and forgot the fire drill. When it came time to make fire and cook food, the woman could not find it.

So they asked Creator about it. Creator went to look for the fire drill himself, and when he got to the place, it had turned into a man.

"All right," said Creator. "Be a man. Be a Russian. Bring tea, sugar, tobacco, salt, hardware, and calico to my people. And let there be fair trade."

Thus it is and has been, they say, ever since.

—Chukchee

The Lizard-hand

The Yokuts Indians of central California say that at first there was nothing but water, with an old stump sticking up out of it—the primeval stump. Some do say it was a mountain top—but this story says it was a stump.

There were several creators. Eagle was the chief one and Coyote was his assistant. Eagle was very wise. Coyote made a lot of mistakes and did some ridiculous things, but he brought about some very good things also.

Coyote was the one who advised Eagle to let Duck dive off the stump and bring up earth from the bottom of the sea to create the world. And Coyote was the one who later stole the sun to make light for the world.

When man was being shaped, Coyote and Lizard argued about the hands.

"The hands shall be like mine," said Coyote, "a good, solid fist."

"No. He needs fingers," said Lizard. "His hand shall be like mine."

Lizard held up his hand. "See!" he said. Lizard had five fingers.

So they argued back and forth. At last Coyote gave in. The man should have a lizard-hand. "All right," he said at last, "but then he will have to die after a while." And that is how man's hand was made and how death came into the world.

—*Yokuts*

How Wisdom Came to Man

Once long ago among the Ashanti people of the old Gold Coast in West Africa, lived Anansi, the spider. He knew everything. He was the wisest one in all the world. *The wisdom of the spider is greater than that of all the world put together* is an old Ashanti proverb.

People used to come to Anansi for advice. They came for help. They used to ask questions, and Anansi knew all the answers.

One day the people offended him in some way, and Anansi decided to hide his wisdom from them and keep it for himself. He even went around picking up the bits he had already given away here and there.

When he had it all together, all the wisdom in the world, he put it in a pot and fixed the lid on tight. Then he hung the pot around his neck, so that it hung down in front of him, and walked off into the forest far from the village. He picked out the highest palm tree he could find and decided to hang the pot in the top of it.

No one could find it there, he thought.

But when he started to climb the tree, the pot hanging from his neck swung between him and the tree, and he slipped down.

He tried again. He climbed halfway up, but again the pot swung in front of him and he slid back.

Again and again he climbed and slipped, climbed and slipped.. But every time the pot hindered him and he could not climb the tree.

It happened just then that Anansi's little son came walking through the forest and saw his father trying to climb the tree with the pot. He watched a while and then called out, "Why don't you hang the pot down your back?"

"That's wisdom!" said Anansi. "I thought I had it all in the pot."

He was so angry that he hurled the pot to the ground. It smashed to bits on a rock, and the wisdom in it got out and flew all over the world.

—Ashanti

46

How Rabbit Stole Fire
from the Buzzards

Nobody had fire in the beginning of time—except the buzzards. The buzzards had fire but they would not share it. In cold weather they used to sit around the fire with their wings spread out. Each buzzard's wings overlapped those of the ones next to him. That way they kept the lovely warmth inside the circle.

One bitter winter day Rabbit was very cold. He was nearly frozen. He came up behind the circle of buzzards and said, "My foot is cold. Can I warm my foot?"

"No," said one big old buzzard.

Rabbit crept around to the other side of the circle.

"My foot is cold!" he cried. "I am nearly frozen."

One buzzard felt sorry for him. "Yes. Warm your foot," he said. He lifted his wing a little and Rabbit crept through to the warmth.

Rabbit really intended to steal a little piece of fire. He had already put pine splinters between his toes. He stretched out his foot to the fire, singing his song of thanks. The splinters caught and blazed up; and Rabbit ran off, leaping and jumping because the fire was hotter than he could bear.

He raced through the woods, jumping, leaping with the pain of the fire. But he was singing his song:

> I am a good rabbit
> I bring fire
> The fire is big and warm
> Now the people will be warm
> The people may sit and be warm.

> *—Catawba*

How the People Got Fire

In the beginning there was no fire. The whole world was cold, until the thunders of the sky struck an old sycamore tree with lightning and put fire in the bottom of it.

Nobody could get it, however, because the tree was on an island, and the fire was inside the tree. Everyone could see the smoke coming out of the old hollow tree, but nobody knew how to get it.

Every animal and bird who knew how to swim or fly offered to go.

They sent Raven first because he was big and strong. He flew across the water and lighted in the top of the tree. He sat there wondering what to do next, and the heat scorched his feathers black. So he flew home. This is why Raven is black today.

Little Wahuhu, the screech owl, went next. He flew across the water to the island and looked down into the hollow tree to see the fire. A blast of hot air puffed up and nearly burned out his eyes. So he had to give up. His eyes are still red today and he can still hardly see in the daytime.

Hoot Owl and Horned Owl went next. The fire was burning hotter and hotter all the time. When they looked down into the tree, the smoke blinded them and the flying ashes made white rings around their eyes. The white rings are still there.

Then little Black-racer Snake said he would go. He swam through the water fast. When he got to the island, he sped through the grass to the foot of the tree. He went into the tree through a small hole in the bottom, but it was so hot in there he had to come out. He was scorched blacker than ever.

Big Blacksnake went next. His name was Climber because he always climbed up the outside of a tree, just as blacksnakes do today. When he poked his head down the tree to investigate the fire, the smoke choked him, and he fell in. It was awful! He climbed out again all right, but he was burned black all over. He too had to go back without fire.

So the birds and the animals and the snakes held a big council. Who would go for fire? Who would know how to get it? Nobody was very eager to go any more.

Finally, Water Spider said she would go. This was not the little water spider that skitters around on top of the water, but the big one with the handsome, black, hairy coat with red stripes. She is very famous. She can run on top of the water and she can dive to the bottom.

"I'll go," she said.

"You can get there, all right," the wise ones answered her, "but how can you carry fire?"

"I know how," she said.

So Water Spider sat down and spun a strong thread. She wove it into a *tusti* (which means bowl), and this she fastened onto her back. Then off she went.

She ran across the top of the water. When she came to the tree, the fire was still burning but beginning to die down. She put one

50

little coal of fire in the tusti bowl and ran back across the water with the tusti on her back.

Everybody was waiting; everybody was watching. They could see a tiny feather of smoke rising from the tusti.

This is how people first received fire, and mankind has used it and kept warm ever since. Water Spider still carries her little tusti bowl today.

—Cherokee

How Man Learned
To Make Fire

In the old first time, people caught fish and ate it raw. They had no fire. Then one day Carancho came among them. As he approached the village, he saw the people eating their meat raw. "I shall teach these people to make fire," he said.

"Who is coming? Who is coming?" the people cried as he came toward them.

"I am Carancho," he said.

"Help us," said the people. "We cannot cook our food."

"You must do as I say," said Carancho.

"Yes, yes!" said the people.

"All right then," said Carancho. "Bring fish."

The people ran and brought many fish.

"Now bring me *pitaladik* and *kuwak'á* wood."

The people brought it.

"Now, watch," said Carancho.

Carancho bored a small hole in the middle of a flat piece of the wood. Then he inserted one end of a long slender stick into an arrow shaft; the other end he inserted in the little hole in the flat stick. Then he twirled the slender stick fast, fast, fast between his hands. Soon the wood smoked; then it glowed. He added tinder and soon had a big fire.

Then the people made more fires and cooked their fish.

—*Toba*

How Mankind Learned
To Make Bread

The first man and the first woman were wandering around under the earth. One day they came upon a pile of millet seed. Then they saw piles of barley and piles of wheat.

"What is all this?" said the man.

Then they saw a little ant running along. The ant stopped and took up one little grain of wheat in its hands. It pulled off the husk and ate the naked grain.

"Kill it! It's ugly! Kill it!" said the woman.

"No," said the man. "It has been created. Just like us it has been created. Watch it."

So the man and woman watched the ant.

"What are you doing?" said the man. "What are these seeds?"

"Do you know what water is?" said the ant.

"Oh, yes," said the man. "We have seen water. Water is for drinking and washing."

"Water is also for cooking," said the ant. "Come with me. I will show you everything."

The little ant led the way to a hole which led from beneath the earth to the surface. "This is my path to the world," said the ant. "Come."

So the first man and the first woman followed the ant up and for the first time saw the face of the earth.

53

"There is the river," he said. "Water for drinking, for washing, and for cooking your grain."

Then the ant said, "Here are stones. Before cooking, you must grind your grain between stones."

Then he showed the man and woman how to lay one stone upon the other; he showed them how to lay the grain between the stones, and how to turn the upper stone so that the grain would be ground into meal.

"This is how," said the ant. He showed them how and helped them do it.

Then he showed the first woman how to make dough with meal and water and how to knead it.

"Next you must have fire," said the ant. He picked up two stones by the river and some dried-up plants and twigs. He struck a spark with flints into the dried kindling, added wood, and soon had a good fire.

"Let the fire grow big and die down to glowing ashes," said the ant to the woman. "Then push it to one side. Lay your flat cakes of kneaded dough in the hot place and cover them up with glowing coals. After a while they will be bread and you can eat it."

The woman did everything the ant said. The first time she brushed the ashes off, the dough was not done; but the second time it was cooked through. It was bread and the man and woman ate it.

—*Kabyle*

ANIMALS

Why the Animals Have No Fire

Long, long ago people had fire. It kept them warm and it cooked their food. But the animals shivered in the forest. They had no fire.

Wolf and Dog were friends in those days. One day Wolf said to Dog, "Go steal a little piece of fire from the people." So Dog, who liked a warm bed, went to the place of the people.

The people liked the dog and threw him bits of food when he came near. So he came nearer. When night came, the people gave him some of their own warm food.

Dog hung around. The people fed him and he forgot all about stealing fire. After a while Dog lived in the house with the people. He slept by the fire and barked if Wolf came anywhere near.

—*Coeur d'Alene: Idaho*

57

How Baboons Came
Into the World

Among the Zulu people, long ago, there were some men who did not like to dig. They did not like to work at all. They said, "We do not have to dig. We can eat the food of others."

They used to lie around and watch other men work. Everybody made fun of them. Everybody ridiculed and despised them so much that one day they decided to go away.

One among them, a man named Tusi, said, "Listen! Get together bread for a journey. We shall go away from here, where there is so much work, far into the forest."

This they did. They got together food for a journey and left that place.

They took along the handles of their hoes and hung them on behind as they walked. Slowly, as they traveled, hair grew on the hoe sticks and they became tails. The men could not pull them off. Hair grew on the men's bodies, and they turned into baboons.

They went to live in the wild rocky places and have stayed there ever since. Now, whenever the people of that old village see a baboon, they say, "There goes one of old Tusi's men."

—*Zulu*

58

Why God Made the Dog

One day God and Saint Peter were walking along and a dog came by. God patted it, and Saint Peter said: "What is that?"

"It's a dog," said God. "Do you want to know why I made him?"

"Yes," said Saint Peter. "What about the dog?"

"Well, you know how much trouble my brother, the Devil, has caused me," said God. "You know how he made me drive Adam and Eve out of Paradise. The poor things nearly starved, so I gave them sheep for meat and warm wool to clothe them. And now that fellow is making a wolf to harry and destroy the sheep!

"So I have made a dog. He knows how to drive the wolf away. He will guard the flocks. He will guard the possessions of man."

—Rumania

Why People Keep Dogs

Once there was a man who went hunting for marsh pigs with his dogs. After a while they startled a marsh pig beside a lake and it fell in.

The man jumped in after it. But a crocodile was in there, too, and the crocodile grabbed him and shoved him into a cave in the bank of the lake.

The dogs could not find their master. They swam around in the lake but could not see him anywhere. They ran back and forth smelling the earth, and at last they scented him through the earth above the cave.

They began to dig. They dug all day and the earth flew. They dug fiercely for three days. When the sun went down on the third day, the man was still in there.

But the dogs did not give up. They dug and dug. Sand began to trickle down on the man's head. He looked up. He saw a crack of light. He heard the dogs.

"My dogs!" he cried. "My dogs have come!"

The dogs heard his voice and dug harder than ever. And at last the man climbed out of the cave through the hole above his head and went home to his village.

60

There he found the people weeping and mourning because they thought he was dead.

"Where have you been?" they said.

So the man told his story. "My dogs saved me," he said. "They searched and dug and found me, and I am here," he said.

"Dogs are good," said the people.

"All men should have dogs," said the man.

"Yes," said the people. "That man's dogs saved his life. Let us have dogs."

Thus the people now keep many dogs.

—*Yao*

Dog's Hoop

The hoop-and-pole game in this story is a famous gambling game for men (usually two) among all Apache Indian tribes. The hoop is rolled along the ground, and, before it falls, the poles are hurled after it. The score depends on the final relative positions of the bands incised on the hoops and poles.

Dog had no possessions. The only thing he owned was a hoop for the hoop-and-pole game. He was always carrying around his hoop; he wanted to play hoop and pole all the time. He was a great gambler, and because he had nothing to wager, he would wager the hoop. And he was always losing it.

The people said, "Let's give him a permanent hoop." So they bent his tail and curled it up over his back like a hoop. And he runs around like that today.

—*Lipan Apache*

62

How People Got the First Cat

The sky in its place; the earth in its place; the four directions as they are. This was the beginning.

A demon lived in a cave somewhere. On fine days he used to let rats run out of the cave. They ran all over and gnawed at Ntzi's skyline and bit it in two. (Ntzi is the high god of the Ch'uan Miao people.)

There were two people in the world at that time, a man and a woman. They slept and then woke up to braid together the sky and the earth where the rats had bitten it. When they had done this, they walked all over the world and looked around. Then they went home and looked around.

The rats were there, eating away at the grain around their house.

Again the two people slept and got up and looked around everywhere. When they got back, the rats had eaten up all the grain around the house and were already eating up the grain in the fields.

"We'd better do something," they said.

So they went to Ntzi and asked him for some cats to catch the rats.

"If you want a cat," said Ntzi, "you'd better go get one from Tiger."

So the man and woman went to see Tiger and asked him for a cat. Tiger handed them a piece of his own liver.

"Is this a cat?" they asked.

"It will be," said Tiger.

So the man and woman turned homeward, and by the time they got home, it had become a cat.

The cat saw the rats and killed them all.

From that day to this, people have had cats, and cats kill rats.

—*Ch'uan Miao*

Why Cat Eats First

One day Cat caught a mouse and was going to eat it when Mouse said, "What! Don't you wash your hands and face before you eat?"

So Cat began to lick her paws and wash her face and make herself nice, as cats do.

While she was busy doing this, Mouse very quietly slipped away. Cat looked around everywhere. No mouse. She looked and looked, but Mouse had gone.

So today Cat eats first and washes afterward.

—*South Carolina Negro*

65

How the First Horse
Was Made

One day Nirantali (the creator goddess of the Konds) sent her brother to get beeswax to make a horse. He brought some and Nirantali, who is also Mother Earth, set to work.

She made the head of the horse first and put two burning coals in it for the eyes. That is why horses today have flashing eyes. She used little pieces of wood for the bones of the back and put four wooden legs on the body. She used lots of wax to stick all the parts together.

"A tail," she said. "A horse must have a tail." So she made a tail out of feathery broom reeds and stuck that on.

The horse was finished and just stood there. Then Nirantali scooped up some dust of the earth and blew it into the mouth and nostrils of the horse. Life swept through it; its eyes glowed; it neighed. Then Nirantali gave the horse to a man and he rode off.

—Kond

Why Goat Cannot Climb a Tree

Once long ago Cat was teaching Goat how to climb a tree. He did not learn in one lesson, but day by day he was learning how.

One day Cat came along to Goat's place and found Goat teaching Dog also how to climb a tree.

"Stop!" said Cat. "Stop that."

"Why?" said Goat.

"You know that Dog is a hunter," said Cat. "If Dog could climb a tree, I would have no safe place to go."

So Cat would not teach Goat any more about climbing trees. He walked off home. And that is why Goat never finished learning how to climb a tree.

—Haitian Creole

67

Why Sheep Does Not
Come In out of the Rain

The sheep hasn't got sense enough to come in out of the rain, so God gave him a thick woolly coat that sheds water. Now he doesn't have to come in out of the rain—doesn't need the sense to, either.

—*North Carolina Negro*

Why Rabbit Has a Short Tail

One day Rabbit was going somewhere and he came to a swamp. It was a big wide swamp. He couldn't swim that far.

Then he saw Alligator. He wondered if he could get Alligator to take him across. He thought Alligator would say No if he asked.

So he said, "Howdy-do, Alligator. I hear you have very few people in your family."

"No, indeed!" said Alligator. "There are lots of people in my family. There are a thousand thousand in my family."

"Call them. I'll count them!" said Rabbit.

So Alligator called them; and they all came!

"Well, how can I count them all mixed up like that!" said Rabbit. "Stand them in a straight line across the swamp."

So Alligator lined them up in a straight line across the swamp.

Rabbit stepped on the back of the first one. "One," he said. "Two —three—four—." Thus he walked across the swamp.

When he came to the last alligator and gave a jump to get ashore, that one bit his tail off! That is why Rabbit has a short tail today.

—*Baganda-Alabama Negro*

How Bat Won the Ball Game

One day the birds and the animals were having a ball game.

Bat came along and wanted to play.

The animals said, "No. You have wings. You belong with the birds." So he went to the birds, and the birds said, "No. You have teeth. You belong with the animals."

Bat went back to the animals. "I have teeth," he said. "I am an animal."

"All right, you have teeth," said the animals. "You can be on our side because you have teeth, but you can't play because you are too little."

So Bat had to watch the birds and the animals play ball. The game started and the birds began to win. The birds could catch the ball as it flew through the air, but the animals could not reach it when it flew too high.

When Bat saw this, he darted into the air and caught the ball, just as old slow-flapping Crane was about to get it. Then in a few minutes he did it again.

Bat was little and fast. He caught the ball again and again, and he won the game for the animals.

"All right, you with the teeth!" said the animals. "You are an animal." Since that day Bat has been counted as one of the animals.

—Creek

70

Why Bat Flies Alone

Once long ago in the war between the animals and birds, Bat was fighting on the side of the birds. In that battle the animals won.

When Bat saw that the animals were winning, he hid under a log and waited. When the battle was over and it was time to go home, Bat went along with the animals.

"What are you coming for?" said the animals. "You were fighting for the birds."

"Oh, I'm not a bird," said Bat. "Look, I have teeth. Whoever saw a bird with teeth?"

So they let Bat come along.

Later the animals and birds had another battle, and Bat was fighting on the side of the animals. This time the birds won the battle.

When Bat saw that the birds were winning, he hid under a log and waited. When the battle was over and it was time to go home, Bat went along with the birds.

"What are you doing here?" said the birds. "You were fighting against us!"

"Oh, I am not one of the animals," said Bat. "Look! I have wings. Animals do not have wings."

So they let Bat come along.

Later on, the animals and birds realized that Bat had joined first one side, then the other. So nobody wanted him.

"Henceforth, you fly alone at night," they said; and that is what Bat does.

—*Modoc*

Why Bear Sleeps All Winter

In the first days of the world, Bear stayed awake all winter just like any other animal.

All the animals thought he was a mean old thing. He was the biggest, so he always had his own way, and the other animals felt put upon. They all felt pretty mad at Old Man Bear a lot of the time.

They called a big meeting one day. All the animals came together to discuss what they could do about Old Man Bear. The meeting went on and on for many days, because nobody could think of what to do.

Then one day Rabbit suddenly remembered that Bear liked to curl up and sleep in a dark, hollow tree.

"Next time let's stop up the tree!" said Rabbit.

All the animals were delighted with this idea. "Maybe he'll take a long nap," they said, "and we'll get some rest."

So they kept watch on Old Man Bear. That night when Bear crawled into a hollow tree to go to sleep, they all worked hard. Everybody brought rocks and boughs and brush and more rocks to stop up the hole in the tree.

In the morning Bear woke up. It was dark in there. He said,

"Sun not up yet," and turned over and went to sleep again. This time he slept on and on in the warm place till spring came and little leaves were unfolding on the trees.

"Do you suppose he's dead?" the animals said to each other. "Didn't he wake up at all?"

Curiosity got the better of them. They had to go peek. So they moved away the rocks and looked in.

There was Old Man Bear sound asleep. When the sunlight poured in on his face, he opened his eyes to little slits and blinked. He stretched; and when he looked and saw the leaves on the trees, he got up and came out in the sun.

"The comfortablest winter I ever had!" said Bear.

Now every year Bear finds a nice warm secret place and curls up and sleeps all winter.

—*North Carolina Negro*

How Chipmunk Got His Stripes

One time long ago, the animals came together to decide whether the world must lie forever in the dark or whether there should be day and sunlight in the world.

Some animals liked the dark night best; some wanted to live in the sun. There was a great discussion.

Bear was one of those who wanted perpetual night.

"Night is best. Let us have darkness," sang Bear. "We must have night," he sang.

Chipmunk was singing too.

"The light will come. Let us have light," he sang. "Let the light come," he sang.

"Night is best. Give us the darkness," sang Bear.

"The light will come!" sang Chipmunk. "Light is coming!" he sang.

He would not give up.

"Light WILL COME!" he sang again.

Just then the sky showed its first surprising red.

Some of the animals ran off at once into the deep woods. Then the fire of the sun's edge rose above the rim of the world.

"Light is coming!" Chipmunk sang.

The sun rose higher and daylight filled the sky.

Bear was very mad. He made a grab for Chipmunk, but Chipmunk got away all right. He ran and popped into a hole in a hollow tree; but—not before Bear's big claws made the marks which are Chipmunk's stripes today.

—Iroquois

Why Lion Lives in the Forest

Long ago the lion was just a big cat that lived with the people. One day he sprang up and killed a chicken and ate it. (The people forgave him. After all, men eat chickens too.)

The next day Lion happened to reach out and scratch the baby.

"Get out of here," the man said, "or I'll kill you."

So Lion ran away into the forest and stayed there.

—*Yao*

How Tiger Learned To Hunt

In the beginning of the world when the animals were learning how to live on this earth, Cat was the smartest one. Tiger noticed this and decided he would ask Cat to be his teacher.

So Tiger went to Cat's house. When he got there, he noticed there was lots of food.

"Do you always have this much food?" said Tiger.

"Oh, yes," said Cat. "Why do you ask?"

"Because I am often hungry. Rabbits and deer are tiger food, they told me, but I cannot catch them because they are agile and swift."

"Well!" said Cat.

"Will you teach me to hunt?" said Tiger.

"Yes, I will," said Cat, "because we are cousins."

"Can we begin right now?" said Tiger.

"All right," said Cat. "The first thing is to pull in your claws so they will never show. Then when you get near your prey, swish your tail around—swish-swish—so he will look at it! Then give a good jump and catch him with your claws. It's easy!"

So Tiger went off, well pleased with the lesson. That is the way Cat and Tiger still hunt today.

—*Popoluca*

How Whale Happens
To Smoke a Pipe

In the beginning, when Kuloskap was still in this world with the Indians and the animals, he used to call the animals to him by singing.

One day when he wished to go across the water from what is now Eastport, Maine, to a place now called Yarmouth, Nova Scotia, he sang for a whale, and a whale came inshore to the song.

Kuloskap stepped upon her back and off they went. When they were almost there, Whale saw the shallow water and was afraid.

"Never mind," said Kuloskap. "Go fast! Go fast."

Whale put on speed and ran aground.

"Oh, my grandson," sang Whale, "what have you done? Now I can never leave the land," she lamented.

"Never fear, Grandmother," said Kuloskap, "you shall swim in the sea again and forever."

He gave her a great push on the head, and she slid back off the flats into deep water.

Then Whale rejoiced.

"Haven't you a pipe and a little tobacco?" she said. "A little tobacco before we part?"

So Kuloskap gave her his pipe and lighted it, and off went Whale happily smoking.

Whale still smokes her pipe today. You can see her puffing her little cloud of white smoke from afar.

—Passamaquoddy

79

Why Elephant and Whale
Live Where They Do

Not in my time, not in your time, but in the old time this story happened. B'Rabby was walking along the shore. He saw Whale.

"Hey! B'Whale," said B'Rabby.

"Hey!" said Whale.

"B'Whale, I could pull you right up ashore," said B'Rabby.

"No, you couldn't," said Whale.

"Bet I can!"

"All right," said Whale and swam off.

B'Rabby was walking along. He saw Elephant.

"Hey!" said B'Rabby.

"Hey!" said Elephant.

"B'Elephant, I could pull you right into the sea," said B'Rabby.

"Who? Me?" said Elephant. "Nobody could."

"I'll do it tomorrow. Twelve o'clock."

Then B'Rabby went and got a lot of rope. The next day he tied one end of it around Whale's neck (but Elephant did not know that). He tied the other end around Elephant's neck (but Whale did not know it).

"When I say PULL, you pull!" he told each one.

"PULL!" he yelled.

80

Whale pulled, and he pulled Elephant down off the land right into the surf of the sea.

"My goodness! Did B'Rabby do that?" said Elephant.

Then Elephant pulled, and he pulled Whale right out of the water up to the edge of the sea into the surf.

Then Whale braced himself against a shelf of rock; and Elephant braced himself against a big tree. Then they both pulled—and the rope broke.

Whale swam away out into the ocean, and Elephant went off into the forest. That is why Whale lives in the ocean today and that is why Elephant stays in the bush.

—*Bahama Negro*

81

Why Spider Has a Little Head
and a Big Behind

Once there was a famine in the village, and Spider (named Kwaku Ananse) went out to find food for his wife.

He went along until he came to a river, and there he saw a lot of water spirits splashing in the water. They were splashing the river dry so they could pick up the fish.

Spider said, "May I splash too?"

"Come," said the spirits.

Spider waded into the river and noticed that the spirits had taken off their heads and were using them to splash with.

"Shall we take off your head so that you too may splash?" they said.

"Please do," said Spider.

So the spirits took off Spider's head and handed it back to him to splash with. They all made big splashings together, and while they splashed, they sang:

> We splash the river dry to catch the fish
> We are using our heads to splash, to splash
> Oh, we are splashing the water.

"I like that song," said Spider. "May I sing too?"

"Sing," said the water spirits.

So Spider sang the splashing song along with the spirits, and there were many fish.

82

When they were finished, the spirits said, "Here is your share," and they gave Spider a big basketful of fish.

"Put your head back on and go home and eat," they said; "but you must never sing that song again or your head will fall off."

"All right," said Spider. "Why should I sing it?" So Spider went off his own way and the spirits ran back into the river.

As Spider was going along happily with his basketful of fish he could hear the spirits singing in the distance. It was the splashing song, and when they came to the lovely high part—*Oh, we are splashing the water*—he forgot and sang it with them.

Right away his head fell off. He could not get it back on by himself, so he ran back to the river.

"I forgot. I sang the song," he said. "Please help me put my head back on."

The spirits fixed Spider's head back on very nicely. Then they said, "If you sing the song again, if your head falls off again, we shall not help you. So good-by."

Spider was very thankful. He started back home again with his basket of fish and his head where it should be. Then once again he heard the spirits singing far away. He liked that song so much that he forgot and sang again. And—his head fell off.

He could not get it back on by himself, but no use to go back. He had to carry it.

This was hard to do. It was very hard to carry the head and that big basket of fish at the same time. So Spider finally clapped the head onto his behind (just to carry it, he thought). But he never got it off again.

That is why spiders today have little tiny heads in front and big behinds.

—Akan-Ashanti

83

How Spider Got His Thread

In the beginning of time and the world, Spider was already there but did not know how to get his food.

He went to see Creator, whose name means Above-Old-Man, and asked him what to do.

"Sit here and work for me a while," said Above-Old-Man; and he gave Spider a string to make.

Spider put the string in his mouth and swallowed and swallowed and swallowed. He kept swallowing.

Above-Old-Man was watching.

All right, he can keep it if he wants it that much, he thought.

All this happened in the sky.

"How shall I get down from here?" said Spider to himself. "There is no way to get down."

So he drew some of the string out of his mouth, tied it to something, and let himself down. He went farther and farther, down and down and down.

At last he came to the earth. Here he used Above-Old-Man's gift of string to make his webs. From then till now Spider catches flies in his web.

—Wishosk (Wiyot)

Why Porpoise Is Not a Fish

Vatea was the great one in the beginning of the world. He was vastness; he was space, the great arch of sky, the first male parent, the first man, and thus the father of men. He was lord of the ocean also, and his shape was half man and half fish.

Vatea's mother was Vari-ma-te-takere. We know nothing about her except that her name means At-the-Beginning.

One day she tore off a piece of her own flesh in order to create the first being. This was Vatea, the first man, but he turned out to be half fish also.

The day Vatea created Taairangi, the porpoise, he imitated the act of his mother. He tore off a piece of his own flesh to create the porpoise and threw it into the sea.

This is why the porpoise is not a fish. He is half man and half fish like mankind's first parent, Vatea.

—Polynesia

Why Dog Gnaws a Bone

Il cane rode l'osso perchè non lopuò inghiothre.
The dog gnaws the bone because he cannot swallow it.
—*Tuscany*

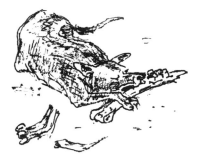

BIRDS

Why the Birds
Are Different Colors

The birds are all different colors today because once, long ago, they flew right into God's rainbow.

You remember how down-hearted poor old Noah was when the flood rains stopped. The raven he sent forth from the Ark to look for dry land never came back. The dove came back all right, with a little leaf in his beak, but he was exhausted and soaked and sodden.

The world was mighty wet out there, Noah thought. He did not dare to let the animals out. He decided to wait a while yet.

So God shoved all the clouds over onto the edge of the world and turned the sun on them. The colors deepened. There was the silver gleam of sun on mist, and through the dazzle shone forth red and green, yellow, orange, blue, deep violet.

The clouds took on the shape of the curving sky over the round earth: an arc with one end on each side of the world. It was God's first rainbow.

The birds were terribly excited. They stuck their heads out the little holes Woodpecker had made for them all around under the edge of the roof. They could hardly wait to get out of there. They thought it was wonderful.

Finally when God called Noah to look at the rainbow and said it was a promise that the rains had stopped, then Noah opened the great big doors of the Ark and let everybody out.

The birds flew out with a great swish of wings and exclamations. They flew right into the rainbow, and through it, and back again.

The ones who flew into the blue color came out blue; the ones who flew into the red came out red. All the yellow birds in the world today are the ones who flew into the yellow.

Some of them were so happy that they flew around and wallowed in the colors, and these today are striped or mottled, or spotted with different colors.

Hummingbird darted around the fastest and the most. He came out with every color of the rainbow on him somewhere.

—North Carolina Negro

Why Chicken Lives with Man

Long ago, as the birds flew over the world, they saw that men had a beautiful thing. It was a bright, blazing thing, very warm. Men cooked their food with it and sat beside it or around it to keep warm.

The birds thought life would be better if they too could have this thing. So they decided to send a messenger to Man to ask him for a little piece of it.

They thought Chicken was a good one to send because he was such a talker. So Chicken went. He flew far over the forest until he came to the towns of men.

He went into a town and walked around. He saw the blazing thing. He learned what it was called. "Fire," he heard men say.

He did not ask for a piece of it to take back to the birds right away, because there was so much food lying around men's dooryards that he started pecking and eating and forgot.

Men liked Chicken because he crowed at daybreak and woke them up. They let him run around in their dooryards and in and out of their houses. They threw him scraps.

So Chicken stayed with mankind. He never went back to the birds. He even forgot how to fly.

—Mpongwe

How Rooster Got His Comb

One time long ago the sun and moon disappeared from the sky. This happened because a hunter shot the moon in the eye with an arrow; then he took another arrow and shot the sun in the eye.

He did this because the sun's light on the moon made a white glare. There was too much light, all day and all night. The glare and the heat withered the mulberry trees.

After this the sun did not rise to shine on the world for three years. The moon too never rose for three whole years. The world was dark. The people could not see. The birds of the air could not find food.

"We shall starve," said the people. "Call back the sun."

Who would know how to call the sun?

"Someone with a loud voice must call the sun," said one old woman.

Cow called, but nothing happened. Cow called eighteen times, but the sun did not answer that bellowing noise.

Then Tiger called to the moon; but Moon was afraid of Tiger's voice.

So time went by. The world was dark. The food plants did not grow; the people could not find food; the birds had nothing to eat.

"Who will call the sun?" cried the people.

So Rooster called.

"That is the right loudness," they said. "Call again. Call back the sun and moon."

So Rooster crowed. The sun peeked up over the edge of the world to see who that was. Rooster crowed again.

"Why, that's my cousin," said Sun.

Rooster crowed again. Sun rose about thirty feet. So Rooster kept on crowing—fifteen, sixteen, seventeen, eighteen times, until the sun and moon were both high in the sky.

The sun was glad to be high in the sky again.

"Thank you," said Sun. "Here! I will give you my comb."

So Rooster took the comb and put it on his head; but he put the back of the comb on his head with the teeth sticking up. He still wears it that way today.

Rooster still crows every morning because he is afraid the sun just might not rise. But it does. It will always come for Rooster's call.

—*Ch'uan Miao*

Why Rooster Is So Neat

Rooster is so neat because he carries a comb.
                              —*United States*

Why Robin Has a Red Breast

One day Robin and his little wife were getting dressed up and discovered that they were all out of camwood powder.

Robin said he would go to the town to buy some, but when he got to the market, all the wonderful camwood powder was gone. He went from trader to trader, but everyone was all sold out.

Robin was so disappointed that finally one trader said, "Here is a little bit. Not enough to sell, just enough to use yourself."

Robin was thankful and put the bit in his mouth to take home to his little brown wife. But the red camwood powder began to melt in his mouth, and as he flew, it dribbled out. No matter how tight shut he held his beak, the precious red paste made streaks around his mouth and dribbled down over his breast.

This is why the robin of the African Congo has a red breast, whereas his wife is a drab little bird with no red on her anywhere.

—*Congo*

How Kingfisher Got His Necklace

Wenebojo was walking along beside a stream. He was sad and angry because his young nephew had fallen into a lake and the underwater people had dragged him down and drowned him.

Wenebojo could not save him, so he was walking along the banks of a stream grieving and full of revenge.

He looked up and saw a bird in a tree watching the water.

"What are you looking for?" said Wenebojo.

"They have drowned Wenebojo's nephew," said the bird. "I am watching for the body to come afloat."

"I have the beads of Wenebojo's nephew," said Wenebojo. "Come here and I'll put his string of beads around your neck."

The little bird came near and Wenebojo slipped the string of white beads around his neck. He was just going to grab the bird, when it darted out of his hand and flew up into the tree.

Wenebojo was angry because it got away. "You will have to dive for a living forever," he yelled. "Your name is Kingfisher."

Today Kingfisher still dives for his food. He still wears the string of white beads around his neck, and his head is bushy because the feathers on the back of his head got rumpled when he escaped from Wenebojo's hand.

—Chippewa

96

How Loon Learned His Call

One time, in the early time, when Kuloskap was hunting on a lake shore in Newfoundland, he saw a loon flying low over the water. Twice the big bird circled the lake, swooping low over Kuloskap on the shore.

"What are you looking for?" called Kuloskap.

"You," said Kwimu, the loon. "Are we friends?"

"Yes," said Kuloskap.

Then Kuloskap taught Loon that day how to call with his own special cry.

"You shall be my messenger," said Kuloskap. "When I need you, I shall call you thus. When you want me, call thus."

This is the beautiful lonely loon's cry we still hear today across some lake or little ocean cove. Since that day loons are faithful to Kuloskap forever.

When the Micmac Indians hear the loon's cry, they still say, "Loon is calling Gluskap." The Passamaquoddy Indians say, "Loon is looning to Kuloskap." But nobody ever knows for sure whether it is Loon calling Kuloskap or Kuloskap calling Loon.

—*Passamaquoddy*

97

Owl

One day Jesus was walking through a small village and went into a baker's shop to ask for bread. The baker's wife picked up some dough, shaped it into a loaf, and put it in the oven to bake for him.

"That's too big for a tramp!" cried the baker's daughter. She grabbed up the newly shaped dough and cut it in half, then put that much back in the oven.

That little piece began to swell and grow. It swelled and swelled, and when it was done, it was the biggest loaf of all.

"Hoo! Hoo!" cried the baker's daughter when she saw it. She was an owl and flew away.

That little hump on the owl's back is said to be a loaf of bread which she has to carry forever to remind her of her stinginess.

—Gloucestershire

Why Wagtail Wags Her Tail

In the beginning Wagtail had no tail. She did not mind very much, but when she was invited to Lark's wedding, she was ashamed to go without a tail.

Wren in those days had a long tail, so Wagtail went to Wren's house and asked to borrow her tail. Wren was kindhearted and quite willing to lend her tail for a few days.

Wagtail, of course, was delighted with the new long tail, and when the wedding was over, she refused to give it back.

So today Wren has only a little upright stump of a tail. Wagtail still has her long one. Every once in a while she wags it to see if it is still there. She is afraid that Wren may come and get it.

—Rumania

99

Why Crow Has a Right
to the First Corn

When Hahgwehdiyu, the Good Creator of Iroquois Indian mythology, first called all the birds to come down from the land of Sun to live on earth, it was Crow who brought the first kernel of corn into the world. Straight from the land of Sun he came with a grain of corn in his ear.

Crow gave it to Hahgwehdiyu, who planted it in the earth to be the life-giving food for man. Thus corn is the gift of Crow to man.

That is why Crow keeps watch over the cornfields. That is why Crow has a right to eat the very first new corn that shows; and that is why he eats the young corn-beetle grubs that go after the roots.

Sometimes people think that crows are digging up the planted grain. The Indians never made that mistake. They knew that when the first little shoots show above ground Corn calls her crows to come and eat the grubs that destroy the roots.

—Iroquois

How Crane Got His Long Beak

One day long ago, in the days of the ancestors, Emu was making a spear, a long, beautiful carved spear with prongs. Nearby Crane was cooking a bandicoot.

It was forbidden in that place for anyone to cook near anyone who was making a spear. So Emu said, "Don't cook here, so close by, because I am making a spear."

This made Crane very angry. He tore up his fire, threw the burning coals at Emu, and flew away. Emu brushed off the coals and took up his spear to throw at Crane, but Crane was already flying in the clouds.

Emu intended to get him, however. He hooked the spear into his spear thrower and took aim. No use! Crane flew into the clouds and Emu could not see him.

Then Emu made a new spear and waited. When at last Crane flew out of the clouds into the open sky, Emu hurled the spear. It was aimed so true that it hit Crane from behind and came out of his mouth.

Crane fell to earth, then tried to pull out the spear. He could not. He pulled and worked at it a long time but could not get it out.

"Oh, well," he said, "I'll leave it there. My children can have it and use it forever."

And so it is. That long beak of Crane's was once Emu's spear.

—Gumaitj

Why Peacock Looks at His Tail

"All's well that ends well," said the peacock as he looked at his tail.

—*Devonshire*

INSECTS, REPTILES, AND FISH

La pulce salta perchè l'è vergognosa.
The flea jumps because he is proud of it.
                                          —*Tuscany*

Why Ants Live Everywhere

All the animals in the forest were going along, on their way to honor the king of the beasts, King Lion.

The ant was among them. He too was going to bow before the king.

It was a hard journey for him. He had to walk over every leaf and stone in the forest. The big animals could leap over things, but the ant had to walk up one side and down the other of everything in the way.

When the little ant arrived—LAST—to bow before King Lion, all the animals laughed at him and drove him away.

The ant went back and told the king of the ants that he had tried to honor King Lion and been driven away and laughed at.

So the ant king sent a worm to go crawl in the lion's ear and bite him.

The lion roared. He rolled. He nearly went crazy; but he could not get the tormenting thing out of his ear. All the animals came running to help him; but not one of them could reach the worm.

At last the lion sent a message to the king of the ants.

"Please send someone," he begged, "to crawl into my ear and pull out this terrible thing."

So the king of the ants sent one of his many people to go tell the worm, "Come out of the lion's ear."

The ant arrived. The lion lay moaning with his chin on his paws. The ant walked up the lion's shoulder. He nearly got lost in the thick tawny mane. But at last he walked into the ear and told the worm, "All right, you can come on out now."

The lion then said that ants had better live everywhere. Today all the other animals live in their own special places in the world. But ants live everywhere.

—*Burma*

Why Ants Carry Large Bundles

One time Anansi, the spider, did something which offended the king. So the king thought up the worst punishment he could imagine. He ordered a big magic box to be made which could never be set down upon the earth.

Anansi, the spider, was then called before the king, accused of his crime, and condemned to carry the box forever. He had to go off into the world carrying the box which could never be set down.

He was soon tired of it. He tried to put it down but could not. Every day he got tireder and tireder and became more and more anxious to get rid of it.

Then one day when Spider was so tired that he could hardly walk, he met Ant.

"Will you hold this box while I go to market?" said Spider to Ant.

"No," said Ant.

"Just hold it till I come back?" begged Spider.

"All right," said Ant, "but hurry."

So Spider handed the box to Ant and he won't take it back.

Today, if you watch, you can see some ant still carrying the big heavy bundle. Sometimes one ant will hand it to another and hurry off. But no ant ever puts it down.

—Ashanti

107

Why Fly Rubs His
Hands Together

In the beginning time, while the people were living at Temecula, Wiyot lay dying there, and the people sent Coyote to find fire with which to cremate his body. He had been poisoned by Frog, who envied his beautiful legs.

Wiyot was the first ancestor and culture hero of the Luiseño Indians, their beloved guardian and teacher.

Coyote ran north looking for fire, but he ran only a little way and came back. They sent him off again. The people had to send him for fire three times more, east, west, south.

The last time Coyote went off, he looked back and saw smoke.

"Why, they've *got* fire!" he said.

Blue Fly had already made it with his twirling stick (his fire drill). Blue Fly twirled the twirling stick so fast between his hands to make fire for Wiyot's mourning ceremony, that today he still does it. That is why flies rub their hands together.

—Luiseño

108

Why Grasshopper
Spits Tobacco Juice

Why does Grasshopper spit tobacco juice? Because he chews tobacco, that's why. Any child can prove this who will pick up a grasshopper gently in his hand. The grasshopper will chew a bit and spit, before you let him go leaping away.

Long ago, Gluskabe used to live with Woodchuck, his grandmother. One day she said, "Grandchild, we are out of tobacco."

"Where shall I get some?" said Gluskabe.

"Grasshopper raises tobacco," said Woodchuck, "but he is stingy; he won't share it."

"I'll get some," said Gluskabe.

Then Gluskabe built a canoe, for Grasshopper lived on an island far off shore. When it was finished, he jumped in and glided out to sea. On the way he wished Grasshopper would not be home, and when he got there, sure enough, Grasshopper had gone off somewhere.

Gluskabe took all the tobacco and piled it into his canoe, then pushed off, and paddled home.

"I have brought tobacco," said Gluskabe. "It will never run out again."

Just then they heard Grasshopper coming. He was paddling fast across the water.

"You took all my tobacco," he yelled.

Gluskabe went to the shore to meet him. "Yes," he said, "I took it all because the people need it forever. You must not be stingy. You must not begrudge tobacco."

"All right," said Grasshopper. "Just give me a few seeds so I can raise some more."

"No," said Gluskabe, "but I will give you enough to last you forever. Open your mouth."

Grasshopper opened his mouth, and Gluskabe put tobacco in it.

"That is your share," said Gluskabe, "enough for forever."

So today Grasshopper still has his tobacco. He chews and spits it all the time.

—Penobscot

Why Crocodile Does Not Eat Hen

Little Hen used to go down by the river every day to pick up little bits of food to eat. One day Crocodile came along and was going to eat her.

"Oh, Brother, don't!" she cried.

Crocodile was so surprised that he did not. He kept wondering why she called him "Brother."

"I'm not her brother!" he said to himself. So he decided that when tomorrow came he would go back and eat the hen.

The next day little Hen was eating by the river when Crocodile came along and was going to eat her.

"Oh, Brother, don't!" she cried.

So Crocodile did not. He began to worry. "How can I be her brother?" he said to himself. He was greatly troubled.

He was going along one day when he met his friend Mbambi, the big lizard. "I'll ask Mbambi," he said.

"Listen, Mbambi," said Crocodile. "A fat little hen comes every day to the river to pick up food, and just when I almost catch her, she says 'Oh, Brother, don't!' so I don't."

"Well?" said Mbambi.

"Why does she keep calling me 'Brother'?"

"Oh, that's easy," said Lizard. "Ducks lay eggs; turtles lay eggs; I lay eggs; you lay eggs; Hen lays eggs. So we are all brothers."

This is why Crocodile does not eat Hen.

—*Fjort*

How Rattlesnake Got His Fangs

In the first days of the world, while all the animals and things and people were people together, they were living at Temecula. Rattlesnake was there. He was one of them.

Everybody made fun of him because he had no arms and legs. North Star was the worst. He even used to throw dirt in Rattlesnake's face and drag him around.

So Rattlesnake went to Earth-Mother and told her how North Star was tormenting him and how all the others laughed.

This was not fair, of course, so Earth-Mother gave Rattlesnake two sharp-pointed sticks and told him to use them against anyone who tried to harm him.

The next time North Star came along and began to abuse Rattlesnake, Rattlesnake put those two sticks to good use. (They were his fangs, of course.) He just bit off one of North Star's fingers.

The Luiseño people used to point to the sky to prove the truth of this story. In the eastern part of the United States you cannot see North Star's hand very well; but all five fingers are visible through the clear air of the Southwest. There is a swirl of little stars about the North Star. A faint line of three or four small stars shows the thumb; four curving lines are the other four fingers. The little finger (which points toward Cassiopeia) is very short, and this is the one that Rattlesnake bit off.

—*Luiseño*

How Tadpoles Lost Their Tails

In the beginning of the world there never was a frog, but there were lots of tadpoles. There were so many tadpoles that you could hardly walk anywhere without squashing them.

So God told them all to go down in the cornfield and pull up weeds.

They went, and they pulled up the weeds for a long time. It was a hot day. The sun shone hot upon them, and they got so tired they could hardly pull up one more little leaf.

The Devil happened to come along just then.

"Nice swimming hole right here," he said.

"We have to pull weeds," said the tadpoles.

"You can pull them faster after a cool swim," said the Devil.

"Well—" said the tadpoles.

"Just look at that water running cool and easy down the creek," said the Devil.

The tadpoles looked.

That did it. They forgot about the weeds. They just made for the water and jumped in. They swam and swam and had more fun than they had ever had before.

That Devil. He went to God and said, "Those fool tadpoles! All they do is swim in the creek. They haven't pulled up a single weed in the cornfield."

So God called the tadpoles and asked them what they had been doing.

"Just swimming."

"Swimming is all right," said God. "I don't mind swimming," he said. "What I can't stand is people not doing what they are told."

So to punish the tadpoles, he cut off their tails.

The tadpoles wept and wailed. "We can't swim without tails," they cried.

"Oh, well, you can swim with legs," said God. "I'll make you some legs."

So God put good swimming legs on the tadpoles, and when he finished the job they were frogs.

This is why tadpoles always lose their tails, and as soon as they do, they are frogs.

—North Carolina Negro

Why Frogs Croak
in Wet Weather

Once there was a young green frog who would not mind his mother. If she said, "Go east," he went west. If she said, "Go up the mountain," he jumped in the river.

After a while the mother grew old and ill. She knew that she was about to die, so she called the young frog to her and said, "When I die, bury me by the river. Do not bury me on the mountain."

She said this because she really wanted to be buried on the mountain. She was sure her son would do just the opposite of whatever she said, as he had all his life.

Finally the old mother died and the green frog was very sad. He was sorry that he had never done what his mother wanted. So this time he was determined to do what she said to do.

Thus the green frog buried his mother beside the river. Then he worried. When it rained he was afraid the waters would rise and wash her grave away; and he would sit on the riverbank and cry with a sad, hoarse voice.

Today green frogs still sit and croak whenever it rains.

—*Korea*

115

How Turtle Keeps
from Getting Wet

One day Turtle climbed up out of his pond and lay on a log in the sun. The sun was warm and it was not long before Turtle was warm and dry.

He raised his head to look around and saw that a rainstorm was coming.

"Oh, dear! I'll get wet!" he cried.

So he jumped—plop—right back into the pond to get out of the rain.

—*Natchez*

Why Flounder's Two Eyes Are
on the Same Side of His Face

Lobster and Flounder were friends and were playing hide and seek. Flounder could always find Lobster because Lobster's antennae always stick up out of any little pool he hides in.

Lobster had a hard time finding Flounder, because Flounder would stir up a cloud of sand or mud, scoot off into it, then turn around and come up alongside Lobster from behind. He did this time and time again.

Lobster got so mad at always being fooled that he jumped on Flounder and stamped him flat.

Flounder cried out with pain. "My eye is in the sand!" he cried. "My eye is in the sand!"

So Lobster fixed that. He picked the eye out and put it on the top side of Flounder.

This is why Flounder is flat and why he has two eyes on the same side of his face.

—Polynesia

Why Jellyfish Has No Shell

Once, long ago, the young bride of the dragon king of Neinya under the sea became very ill. No one knew what was the matter. Doctors came to see her but none could cure her. Priests and diviners were called in but could not name the trouble.

Finally the young girl herself said, "If I could just have some raw monkey liver, I could get well."

So the sea-dragon king called Jellyfish.

"Go to the land," he said, "and bring back a monkey here. You are the only one who can go, for you have legs."

118

In those old days Jellyfish had legs and a tail and a good thick shell on his back.

Faithfully he swam and swam until he came to a sandy island. He walked ashore and saw a monkey playing in a pine tree.

"This is a dry hot place," said Jellyfish. "You ought to see Neinya, the beautiful kingdom of fruit and jewels under the sea. How would you like to go there?"

Well, yes. Monkey thought he would like to go to see those wonders.

"All right. Get on my back," said Jellyfish.

So Monkey came down from his tree and sat on Jellyfish's hard-shelled back. Off they went.

About halfway there, Jellyfish suddenly said, "I do hope you brought your liver with you."

Monkey was astounded at the question.

"Why do you ask?" he said.

"Well," said Jellyfish, "our young sea-dragon queen is very ill, and nothing but monkey liver will cure her."

"Oh," said Monkey, "why didn't you tell me?"

"Because then you wouldn't have come."

"On the contrary!" said Monkey. "You see, I have two livers, and I'll gladly give the young queen one of them. But the trouble is," he added, "I left them both hanging in the pine tree. Let's go back and get one."

"Nothing else to do!" said Jellyfish. So he turned around and swam back to the monkey's island.

Monkey hopped ashore and leaped up into the highest branches of the tree.

"Liver, liver, liver!" he yelled. "You can't have mine!"

So Jellyfish swam back to Neinya and told the story. The old sea-dragon king was furious.

"Stupid!" he cried. "Stupid!—Beat him to jelly!" he cried to those around him.

So the officers of the court beat up the jellyfish. They knocked off his legs and his tail and smashed his shell. Thus to this day Jellyfish has no legs and no tail and no shell. He is just jelly.

—Japan

Why Crab's Eyes Stick Out

One day Nzambi (the Old Mother Earth of the Fjorts) had gone to a certain town to settle some palaver; and while they were "talking the palaver," Nzambi heard a drum. It sounded like the drum in her own town, and she wondered what was the matter there. She sent the pig to find out.

(A palaver is an argument which has sprung up between two or more persons and has led to a quarrel. Some are very silly or simple; some are very serious, such as those which involve bloodshed or intertribal disputes. All require judicial settlement and must be talked out before some chief or prince.)

The pig went but saw no one beating Nzambi's big drum. He came back and said all was quiet in the town.

"But I heard my drum," said Nzambi.

The palaver continued, and again while they were talking, Nzambi heard her own great drum.

"Go, Antelope," said Nzambi, "go see who dares to beat Nzambi's drum."

The antelope went. He saw nothing; he heard nothing. He came back. "Nothing," he said.

The palaver was almost over when Nzambi heard her drum again.

"Come!" said Nzambi. "We'll all go."

When they all came home to Nzambi's town, they saw nothing, heard nothing.

"Hide in the grass," said Nzambi. "Wait! Watch."

So they hid themselves and waited. After a while they saw Crab come out of the water. They watched. They saw Crab creep sideways up to Nzambi's drum and beat it. At the mysterious sound his eyes popped out and Crab sang:

> Nzambi has gone up the mountain.
> I'm all alone.

Then the people all jumped out and grabbed him and took him to Nzambi.

Nzambi said, "You have behaved as if you had no head, so now you shall live without a head forever."

Thus Crab has no head, but Crab can still lift his eyes up out of his body in order to see.

—*Fjort*

PLANTS

Why Some Trees Are Evergreen

When the plants and trees were first made, they were told to stay awake and keep watch for seven nights. They tried to do this, and all of them stayed awake all night the first night.

On the second night they all tried to stay awake, but a few fell asleep before morning. On the third night a few more fell asleep. (Staying awake for seven whole nights is very hard to do.) On the fourth night the trees were still trying to stay awake, but once again a few more of them slept.

By the time the seventh night came, the only trees and plants that managed to keep awake were the cedar, the pine, the spruce, fir, holly, and the laurel.

These were the only ones who stayed awake the whole seven nights of the testing time.

"You have endured," someone said. And to these was given the gift to be forever green. All the other trees and plants lose their leaves and sleep all winter.

—*Cherokee*

125

How the Coconut Tree
Was Saved

Long ago there was a flood. The waters rose; people and animals were drowned. Even the mountains were covered with water— all except one. The top of the very highest mountain in the world still stuck up in the air.

The top of that mountain was certainly crowded. All kinds of people and animals were huddled together on it: cats, pigs, dogs, all sorts of others. Some were still floating or swimming in the water around the mountain peak because there was no room.

A man saw a cat afloat on a coconut, bobbing along in the water.

"Hello, dear cat," said the man. "Give me that coconut."

"No," said the cat. "This is the only plant left in the world."

"I'll plant it and take care of it for us both," said the man.

"No," said the cat; and he clung to the precious, floating thing.

After a while the waters began to go down. First the mountain peaks appeared; every day more and more of the mountain sides were bared. Finally patches of flat wet earth lay steaming in the sun.

The coconut settled on the earth. It took root and grew into a tall tree. The man came along, and the cat and the man lived together. They took care of the coconut tree and ate coconuts.

Today both cats and men still love coconuts.

—*Apayao*

How Bean Got His Stripe

One day a bean, a long straw, and a glowing coal found themselves together in a dangerous predicament. The straw and the coal had just escaped being burned up in a blazing fire. The bean had fallen out of a boiling pot, which hung over it.

"What shall we do now?" said the coal.

"Well, this is no place for any of us," said the bean. "Let's travel."

"A fine idea," said the other two. So they started out.

After a while they came to a running brook and did not know how to get across. Straw was afraid of being swept away by the current. Coal was afraid she would sink. Bean could not swim.

"I shall lay myself across the brook, like a bridge," said Straw, "and you can walk over."

So Straw stretched and stretched until he touched the other side of the brook and lay there, like a little bridge. "Come on," he said.

Coal started first and trotted over until she heard the running water. Then she was frightened and just stood there. Of course, this made the straw catch fire. It burned and broke and fell in the brook, and the coal too fell into the water and sank with a sharp hiss.

Bean was watching, and Bean laughed. Bean laughed and laughed until he split his sides! That could have been the end of Bean, too, if a tailor had not happened along just then and sewed him up.

You can still see those seams in every bean today.

—Europe

How Yams Got Their Eyes

One day a red flying bird with his hat and his long beak flew over the garden of Rapu, the great gardener of Easter Island mythology. Rapu owned all the plants in the world except one. He had no yams.

Rapu looked up and saw the bird. "Can you find yams?" he said.

The bird flew west and west with his hat and his long beak, until he saw an old man digging out yams in a little garden.

He saw that one big red yam had rolled aside. He watched and when the old man turned his head, he stuck his long beak deep into the big red yam and flew away.

The yam owner heard the sound of wings; he turned his head and saw the bird flying off with the yam.

"Fly straight on," he cried.

So the bird flew straight on and came back to the garden of Rapu. He dropped the yam into the cut earth, where it took root and put out leaves and lived and grew.

Today when Easter Islanders dig their yams and see the little eyes on them, they say, "That is where the red flying bird with his hat stuck in his long beak."

—Easter Island

CONSTELLATIONS

The Great Bear

When the old Micmac Indians used to look up in the sky in late spring, they saw the big bear crawl out of her cave and start across the heavens. All summer she runs across the northern sky with seven hunters after her.

The cave is the beautiful little arched constellation called Corona Borealis. The four stars of the Dipper represent the bear. The three stars in the handle are the first three hunters: Robin, Chickadee, Moosebird. Four more hunters follow them but cannot keep up. We can see them all summer, but they drop out of sight below the horizon in the fall.

Robin is the first hunter (his star has a reddish tinge). Not far behind comes Chickadeé, carrying his little pot to cook the meat. (This is the double star in the middle of the handle; the little star Alcor is the pot.) The third hunter is Moosebird, who is never very far behind successful hunters.

Pigeon is the next hunter, and after him comes Bluejay (whose star is blue). Next comes the big owl (the star Arcturus in Boötes) and below him little Saw-whet (the tiny Acadian owl).

The two owls are the first to drop out of the chase—Saw-whet because he is too small to keep up with the hunters, the big owl (Arcturus) because he is too heavy. Pigeon and Bluejay get lost and give up; they drop below the horizon also.

But Robin and Chickadee follow the bear, and Moosebird follows the hunters. Robin kills the bear with an arrow, and she slowly falls over on her back. Her blood spatters Robin's breast, staining it red forever. The blood drips down to earth on the Nova Scotia maples. That is why they turn to gorgeous red every fall.

Chickadee and Robin cook the meat in the little pot, and Moosebird arrives, just as he does today in the Canadian woods right after some hunter has killed a moose or a bear or some other animal. Even though he is late and did not help, Robin and Chickadee share their meat with him. All good Micmacs have always shared their food with those who have none.

The old dead bear lies on her back all winter, but her spirit returns to the cave to sleep the winter through. And a new bear, reborn, comes forth every spring to flee before the hunters and re-enact this drama forever and forever.

—*Micmac*

Why People Watch the Dipper

Long ago this happened, when the Dipper in the sky called down to the people and said, "Watch me, my grandchildren!"

"Watch me," he said. "As long as you see me going around, around, around, all shall be well with you."

So the people watched.

"If the moon gets lost, never mind," said Dipper. "Moon is always getting lost and coming back; but if I get lost, I can never come back. So watch me, my grandchildren."

Whenever there is an eclipse of the moon, the people wait, because soon Moon slips out again from behind the dark shadow. But everybody knows that if ever the Dipper disappears from the sky, that will be the end of the world.

This is why the Indians watch the Dipper faithfully.

—*Tahltan*

135

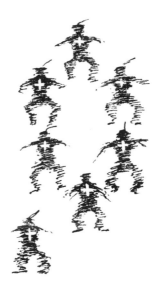

Pleiades

Long ago when the world was new (as the Cherokee Indians say), there were seven young boys who used to play together all the time. Their favorite game was the *gatayû'sti* game. (This is the famous wheel-and-stick game of many southern tribes, played by rolling a stone wheel along the ground and sliding a stick along after it. See p. 156.)

They played all the time. They were always late for meals; they never wanted to help in the cornfield. They never wanted to do anything but play the gatayû'sti game. All the mothers scolded them, but it never did any good.

So one day the mothers got together some of the gatayû'sti stone wheels and boiled them in the pots with the corn for dinner. When the boys finally showed up, the mothers dipped out the stones and said, "Late again! Since you love gatayû'sti better than corn, here are the stones for your dinner."

136

The boys were very angry. They ran out of the houses and all ran back to the playing field together.

"Our mothers are mean," said one.

"I'm never going back home," said another.

"Let's all go away from here," said another boy.

"Let's all go where we can't trouble them any more."

So they began to dance. Round and round and round in a circle the boys began their dance together.

"Let us go far," they sang; and they prayed to the spirits for help.

As they danced they noticed that they were whirling faster and faster and that their feet were not touching the ground. They did not care; they went right on dancing—round and round.

Finally, when the boys did not come home, the mothers got worried and went out to look for them. They saw their children dancing down by the playing field. They called, but the boys did not answer. They watched and saw that their feet were not touching the ground. And now, with every round, they seemed to rise higher and higher into the air.

The mothers ran and tried to grab their feet and save the children, but it was too late. The dancing boys circled higher and higher until they reached the sky. There they became the bright little constellation we call the Pleiades. The Cherokee Indians call it *Ani'tsutsa,* which means "the Boys."

—*Cherokee*

137

Udleqdjun in the Sky

One day three men went bear hunting on the ice with dogs and sledge, and they took a young boy along to help them. They went far out on the ice field. As they neared the edge of the floe, they saw a bear and went after him.

The dogs ran fast but the bear ran faster. They could not catch up. Then suddenly the bear seemed to be lifted up. Men, dogs, and sledge rose into the air also, still following the bear, but could not catch him.

The boy lost one of his mittens and fell off when he leaned over to reach for it. He stood and watched the bear and the hunters rise higher and higher into the air and finally become stars.

The bear star is named Nanuqdjung (*nanuq* means bear). This is the star we call Betelgeuse in the constellation Orion. The three hunters are the three bright stars we call Orion's belt. The Eskimos named the constellation for them: "following one another," or Udleqdjun. The sledge (Qamutiqdjung) is represented by the stars we see as Orion's sword.

There they are today: three hunters with their sledge and dogs following the bear. The boy who fell off is not with them. He went home and told this story.

—Central Eskimo

Notes and Bibliography

The motif numbers are from Stith Thompson's *Motif Index of Folk Literature. Abbreviations used in the notes and bibliography:*

BAEB—Bureau of American Ethnology Bulletin
BAER—Bureau of American Ethnology Annual Report
BPBMB—Bernice P. Bishop Museum Bulletin
DFML—Standard Dictionary of Folklore, Mythology, and Legend
ERE—Encyclopedia of Religion and Ethics
FMNHP—Field Museum of Natural History Publication
JAF—Journal of American Folklore
MAAA—Memoirs of the American Anthropological Association
MAFS—Memoirs of the American Folklore Society
MAR—Mythology of All Races
ODNR—Oxford Dictionary of Nursery Rhymes
PAES—Publications of the American Ethnological Society
SMC—Smithsonian Miscellaneous Collections
UCPAAE—University of California Publications in Anthropology, Archaeology, and Ethnology

Earth, Sky, and Sea

What Makes Moonshine on Water. This is a Mexican nursery rhyme explaining the moon's reflection in a lake. See A. S. Gatchet, "Popular Rimes from Mexico," *JAF* 2: 50.

Who? This story of the beginning of the world is a story told by the Yuchi Indians of eastern Tennessee to the Creeks, their Georgia, South Carolina, and Florida neighbors, with whom they united for the protection of numbers after the coming of the white man. It is based on the myth in the W. O. Toggle Collection in the Bureau of American Ethnology, presented by John R. Swanton: "Myths and Tales of the Southeastern Indians," *BAEB*, 88: 84–85.

How the Earth Was Made To Fit the Sky. This myth is told by the Bugun people (often called Khowa) of the former North-East Frontier of India, a wild area in the Himalaya mountains of Assam. As told here, it is based on the telling reported by Verrier Elwin: *Myths of the North-East Frontier of India*, p. 9.

The myth contains two etiological motifs: making the earth smaller—A852, and creation of mountains and hills by the god's hand—A962.2. In addition to this Bugun tale there are Jewish, Rumanian, and Finnish stories in which the mud that spurted out from between God's fingers (when he squeezed the earth to make it smaller) became the mountains.

The Angami people of Assam also tell a brief myth embodying both these motifs:

In the beginning the earth was too big. The sky could not cover it. Sky said to Earth, "You are too big. Wrinkle up your feet a little."

So Earth wrinkled up her feet until she fit the size of the sky. That is why there are mountains and hills and valleys on the face of the earth (those wrinkles) and why the sky is smooth.

Hills because Sky asked Earth to wrinkle up her feet is motif A969.4. The tale is published in Elwin: *Myths of the North-East Frontier of India*, p. 16n6, citing J. H. Hutton: *The Angami Nagas of Assam*, London, 1922, p. 260.

For motif A961.1—hills created from flapping of wings of primeval bird, see the Yuchi Indian story "Who?" in this book, p. 15.

How the Sun Was Made. This is a story of the Euahlayi people on the Narran River in New South Wales, Australia. As told here it is slightly condensed and simplified from the version in K. Langloh Parker: *Australian Legendary Tales*, pp. 21–23. Sun as fire rekindled every morning is motif A712. See "How Rooster Got His Comb," (pp. 92 and 93) for analogs. See also *DFML*, 579b.

Why Sun and Moon Live in the Sky. This is a cosmological myth of the Efik people of southern Nigeria, condensed from the telling in E. Dayrell: *Folk Stories from Southern Nigeria*, pp. 64–65.

How the Earth's Fire Was Saved. This is a myth of the Tinguian people of north-western Luzon, P. I., based on Fay-Cooper Cole: "Traditions of the Tinguian," *FMNHP* 180: 189 #63. Escape from deluge is the subject matter of motifs A1012–A1029.6, but all these are concerned with the detailed accounts of lone or paired human survivors.

How the People Sang the Mountains Up. This story is greatly simplified and greatly condensed from the long origin and emergence myth of the Jicarilla Apache Indians of southwestern Colorado and northern New Mexico, in the collection made by Dr. Marvin E. Opler in 1934–1935. See his "Myths and Tales of the Jicarilla Apache Indians," *MAFS* 31: xv, 1, 11–13, 16–19, 26, 164, 164n1. It is one of the outstanding myths in all North America exemplifying the creative and compulsive power of song. See Introduction, p. 11.

The emergence myth is important in North American Indian mythology, especially among tribes of the Southwest: the Apache groups, the Pueblo groups, the Navahos, the Pimas. See *DFML*, 344bc, 669b. It occurs occasionally in, but is not a feature of, other North American areas. Emergence of tribe from lower world is motif A1631. Mankind emerges from mountain is motif A1234.1 and refers specifically to the Pijao Indians of Colombia—one of several tribes of Colombia and Ecuador who attach religious importance to their emergence myth and venerate the sacred emergence mountain. See *BAEB* 143:5:724.

Why the Tides Ebb and Flow

1. Tahltan. North American Indian tide-origin tales (motif A913) usually involve a culture hero who wrests the tides from some impounder or custodian who prevents their ebb and flow. This Tahltan Indian tale is based on the text given by James A. Teit: "Tahltan Tales," *JAF* 32: 201, 218, 219. Franz Boas reports a tale from the last Ts'ets'ā'ut Indians of Portland Inlet between Alaska and British Columbia, in which the culture hero (named Qā) dug a hole himself for the sea to pour in and out of and set a guardian over it to regulate the ebb and flow. See Franz Boas: "Traditions of the Ts'ets'ā'ut," *JAF* 9: 258–259 (1896), citing his own book *Sagen der Indianer der Nordpacifischen Kuste Amerikas*, p. 313.

In Europe, however, the tides are usually explained as having been caused by some wading sea-god or giant. In Greek mythology, for instance, Orion waded across the Aegean Sea, thus causing the tides. The huge Celtic Bran caused the tides to rise when he walked through the Irish Sea between Britain and Ireland to rescue his sister. The Old Norse god Thor was also a tide raiser in the Baltic. The ancient Danish sea giant Wade, too, waded the deep Grönsund channel between Falster and Möen Islands in the Baltic, thus causing the tides to rise and fall ever since.

2. Malay. This brief myth from the Malay Peninsula is based on W. W. Skeat: *Malay Magic*, pp. 6–7, 92. See also *DFML*, 1113a.

Why the Sea Is Salt.
This is a condensation of the myth as given in Snorri Sturluson: *Prose Edda*, pp. 161–169. Why the sea is salt is motif A1115.2, citing this Eddic reference plus one Chinese reference. It represents roughly the old myth of the *Prose Edda*: magic mill stolen by sea captain, who orders it to grind salt. He cannot stop it; ship sinks under weight of salt; mill still grinding salt. The self-grinding salt mill is motif D1601.21.1, citing references to tales known across northern Europe: in Germany, Denmark, Norway, Sweden, Finland, Lapland, Estonia. The motif turns up in *Grimm's Fairy Tales*, #103; and Keigo Seki reports fourteen versions of the stolen salt-grinding millstones from Japanese oral tradition. See his *Folktales of Japan*, pp. 134–138. There are also tales explaining why the sea is salt from Holland, Hawaii, New Guinea, and from the Tupinamba Indians of Brazil.

Who the Man in the Moon Is

1. The Old Man and His Bush. This is a myth of the Altai Tatars of Siberia, based on the story as given by Uno Holmberg: "Siberian Mythology," *MAR* 4:423–424, 424n23, citing G. N. Potanin: *Očerki sěvero-zapadnoy Mongolii*, vol. 4, Petrograd, 1883, pp. 190–191. Motifs A751–A751.11 (35 motifs inclusive) deal with man-in-the-moon concepts and cite references to tales found widely throughout the British Isles and Europe (e.g., in Germany, Brittany, France, Flanders, Denmark, Estonia, Livonia, Finland, Lithuania, Rumania, plus Old Norse, or Icelandic, and Jewish tales). There are also tales from Siberia, Armenia, China, Japan, India, from North American, Central American, and South American Indians, from African and U.S. Negroes, and from Oceania (Hawaii, Tuamotu, Samoa, Tonga, New Zealand, and Philippine Islands).

2. *The Old Humpback.* This story from the Malay Peninsula is based on the version given in W. M. Skeat: *Malay Magic,* p. 13. See also *DFML,* 672c. Skeat also cites a brief Sanskrit myth (p. 13*n*2) which explains the spots on the moon's face as a hare (or an antelope). It was fleeing in terror from a hunter and prayed to the moon for protection. The moon took up the frightened thing in her arms. And there it is. Man in the moon as hare (or other animal) is motif A751.2.

3. *Frogs in the Moon.* This story of the Lillooet Indians follows the version given by J. A. Teit: "Traditions of the Lillooet Indians of British Columbia," *JAF* 25: 298. Frog in the moon is motif A751.3, citing a tale of the South American Warrau Indians. Motif 751.3.1 is man in the moon is a frog (frogs) which has jumped into his face and remains there. Stith Thompson: *Tales of the North American Indians,* Harvard University Press, Cambridge, 1929, p. 291*n*69, cites this Lillooet tale and similar tellings from nineteen other North American Indian tribes.

4. *Hjuki and Bil.* This ancient little anecdote occurs in Snorri Sturluson's *Prose Edda,* Gylfaginning, 11. Two children on moon with yoke and bucket is motif A751.7, citing J. A. MacCulloch, "Eddic Mythology," *MAR* 2: 184, Boston, 1930. The foremost exponent of the Jack and Jill speculation seems to have been Rev. Sabine Baring-Gould: *Myths of the Middle Ages,* Rivingtons, London, 1866, pp. 188–190. The idea appealed to scholarly imagination in the last half of the nineteenth century and was widely popular although never unconditionally accepted. See I. and P. Opie: *ODNR,* 225–226; Brian Branston: *Gods of the North,* Thames and Hudson, London and New York, 1955, pp. 70, 300; *DFML,* 672c

5. *The Moon's Face.* This small myth is sketched by E. N. Fallaize in the article **sun, moon, and stars,** *ERE* xii: 62b, citing A. C. Hollis: *The Masai: Their Language and Folklore,* Oxford, 1905. See also *DFML,* 672c.

Man

How the People Began. This is a Greenland Eskimo story collected from the Smith Sound group by Knud Rasmussen, the famous Danish explorer who was himself part Eskimo: condensed from the recording given by him in his *Eskimo Folk-Tales,* pp. 16–17.

The interesting belief that stars are souls of the dead is not limited to the Greenland Eskimos. The belief is as old as ancient Egypt and has been reported from Siberia, from several Shoshonean Indian tribes of California, and also from the northeastern Penobscots. It comprises motifs E741.1 and E741.2. The latter represents a Mandan Indian concept that when a star falls, the soul is being reborn and will reappear as a star in the sky when it dies again. Among the Fox, Delaware, and Shawnee Indians, stars were believed to be the souls of the dead and were called "grandfathers." See also *DFML,* 100b, 487b, 1009d, 1051a, 1081c.

Chameleon Finds—. This story, told by the Yao people who live along the shores of Lake Nyasa in northern Mozambique, is rewritten from Duff Macdonald's literal transcription of it as told to him and published in his *Africana, or the Heart of Heathen Africa,* vol. 1, 295f.

Creator Makes—. This is a creation myth of the Chukchee people of northeastern Siberia, told to Dr. Waldemar Bogoras by a Reindeer Chukchee man on the Omolon River in 1895. This region is now part of the Yakutok Republic in Soviet Russia. As told here, the story follows, greatly condensed, the English translation given in Waldemar Bogoras: "Chukchee Tales," *JAF* 41: 298–300.

That the Russians originated from a fire drill left behind at an old Chukchee camp is a widespread tale among the Chukchees. Dr. Bogoras thought the concept probably sprang from a pun on the Chukchee and Russian words for fire drill. See Bogoras, p. 300n2.

The Lizard-hand. This story is based on material in A. L. Kroeber: "Handbook of the Indians of California," *BAEB* 78: 510f., and the lizard-hand incident in Stith Thompson: *Tales of the North American Indians,* from Kroeber: *University of California Publications in American Archaeology and Ethnology* 4:231 (1907). The lizard-hand is motif A1311.1.

How Wisdom Came to Man. This is a myth of the Ashanti people of the old West African Gold Coast, condensed from the telling in Barker and Sinclair: *West African Folk-Tales,* pp. 33–34.

Anansi, the spider, is both creator and culture hero in much West African mythology; but his star role is that of trickster—crafty, shrewd, selfish, clever—who makes his way in the world by his wits against great odds. Sometimes he gets into trouble, but he always gets out of it by turning himself into a little household spider. For the regional and cultural spread of Anansi as creator–culture hero–trickster, see *DFML,* 18d, and the article "Anansi," 52d–53a. The Nigerian Yoruba people have a similar tale in which Tortoise is the collector and hider of wisdom and a passing hunter (instead of a child) is the observer and adviser. See P. Itayemi and P. Gurrey: *Folktales and Fables* (West African Series 3), Penguin Books, London, 1953, pp. 92–93.

Origin of human wisdom is motif A1481, which parallels a group of tales about the impounding (by a monster or trickster or some selfish character) of water, of foods, game animals, etc., which are either liberated by a culture hero for the benefit of mankind or escape in some way to take their place in the order of life on earth.

How Rabbit Stole Fire from the Buzzards. This is a story of the Catawba Indians of South Carolina, following the text collected by Frank G. Speck: *Catawba Texts,* pp. 8–9.

How the People Got Fire. This fire myth of the Cherokee Indians is based on the text collected by James Mooney: "Myths of the Cherokee Indians," *BAER* 19, Pt. 1:

240–242. The successful fire bringer, Water Spider, with her little *tusti* bowl, was identified by Mooney (p. 430, 431) as *Argyroneta aquatica,* a large hairy species which not only runs across the water but dives and also weaves for itself a little underwater dome-shaped house, of which the upper half is filled with air. The word *tusti* in Cherokee means "little bowl."

Stories about how mankind got fire circumnavigate the globe from the Baltic to India, to Australia. The basic and most usual myth is the theft of fire by a culture hero (A1415); it is often stolen from some specific person or animal (A1415.0.2) by an animal (A1415.2) or bird (A1415.2.1). Often it is deposited in a tree, or trees, so that mankind can find and release it (A1414.7.1). The tales have been told and recorded with local variations and differing environmental details by such wide-spread peoples as the ancient Persians, Hindus, Greeks, Finns, Lithuanians. Both African and New World Negros have innumerable theft-of-fire myths. Polynesian, Melanesian, Micronesian fire myths and those of certain Australian groups also follow these patterns. Almost every North American Indian tribe has a fire myth as do most South American Indian tribes and Mexican and Central American Indian peoples.

In nearly all instances the fire thief, whether successful or unsuccessful, bears the mark of that exploit forever: robin's red breast reflects his fire-stealing adventure, for instance (A2218.5); and so does the little burnt spot under rabbit's chin (A2218.7). In this Cherokee story, Raven's feather's are scorched black; Screech Owl's eyes are burnt red; Blacksnake gets scorched completely black.

How Man Learned To Make Fire. This myth about the fire drill is one collected by Alfred Métraux among the Toba and Pilagá Indians during his two expeditions into the Argentine Chaco in 1933 and 1939. See Alfred Métraux: "Myths of the Toba and Pilagá Indians of the Gran Chaco," *MAFS* 40: 3, 54–56.

Carancho is the wise and beneficent culture hero of the Toba Indians; he exterminated all monsters and all cruel people, showed men how to make and use the fire drill, how to hunt game, make weapons, and cure the sick. His name means "hawk" and refers specifically to the South American caracara (*Polyborus plancus*), a strong, fearless, long-legged, vulture-like hawk.

For the woods used by Gran Chaco tribes to make the fire drill, see A. Métraux: "Ethnography of the Chaco," *BAEB* 143: 1: 299. Fire drill invented is motif A1414.-1.1, citing myths from India, from certain California Indians, from the African Bushongos, and from the South American Kaskiha and Toba Indians.

The origin of fire by rubbing sticks together (motif A1414.1) is attributed sometimes to Prometheus, sometimes to Hermes in the classic mythology of the ancient Greeks. See *DFML,* 389b. There are also Jewish, Kaffir, and Polynesian origin tales for the origin of fire by rubbing sticks together.

How Mankind Learned To Make Bread. This story is condensed from the long creation myth collected by Leo Frobenius among the Kabyle people of the Djurdjura mountains of northeastern Algeria during his 1912–1914 expedition and published in Leo Frobenius and D. C. Fox: *African Genesis,* pp. 57–61 (first published in his *Atlantis: Volksmärchen and Volksdicktung Africas,* vol. 1, Jena, 1921).

146

It is interesting to note that in the mythology of the Jicarilla Apache Indians of New Mexico grasshopper is custodian of wheat and made bread baked in ashes. See M. E. Opler: "Myths and Tales of the Jicarilla Apache Indians," *MAFS* 31: 15, 94, 177–179.

Animals

Why the Animals Have No Fire. This is a story of the Coeur d'Alene Indians, an inland Salishan tribe of northern Idaho, collected by Dr. Gladys Reichard in 1929, and reported in her "An Analysis of Coeur d'Alene Myths," *MAFS* 41: 193–194. The same story is also told by their neighbors, the Cowlitz, Humptulip, and Quinault tribes of the Coast Salish on the coast of Washington. Among the Quileute Indians of the coast of Washington, it is Snowbird who goes for fire and does not return. In the Quinault tale, Robin and Dog both go and neither return.

Motif A2433.3.2 cites an Angola tale explaining that Dog sleeps by the fire because he was "seduced with mush." See Leach: *God Had a Dog*, 199–200, citing Chatelain: "Folk-Tales of Angola," *MAFS* 1: 213.

How Baboons Came Into the World. This is a story of the Zulu people of Natal, South Africa, based on the version as given by Henry Callaway: *Nursery Tales, Traditions, and Histories of the Zulus*, pp. 178–180. There is a group of Zulus known as the Amatusi (which means "people of Tusi") who recognize baboons as their descendants.

Creation of baboon is motif A1863 citing the Zulu tale and one from the Ila-speaking people of Northern Rhodesia.

It is interesting to note that the Tinguians of northwestern Luzon, Philippine Islands, have a monkey-origin story (motif A1861) very much like this.

Once there was a very lazy man planting grain. He would plant a few seeds, then he would stick his planting stick upright into the ground and lean back on it to rest. He did this so often and rested so long that the stick grew onto his behind like a tail. Then he was a monkey forever after. See F.-C. Cole: "Traditions of the Tinguian," *FMNHAS* 14, p. 189.

A Bagobo story from Mindanao, P. I., also states that monkeys were originally men, but the transformation seems to have been accidental, not punitive, in this tale: a man climbing on a roof held in his hand a ladle made of coconut shell. He held it behind him as he climbed. It stuck there, became a tail, and the man was a monkey henceforth. See L. W. Benedict: "Bagobo Myths," *JAF* 26: 24 (1913).

The Mocovi Indians of the Gran Chaco in South America say that once a great fire destroyed the world long, long ago, and all the people were destroyed except one man and one woman, who fled into the tops of tall trees and stayed there. Their faces got singed, however, and they became monkeys. See A. Métraux: "Myths of the Toba and Pilagá Indians of the Gran Chaco," *MAFS* 40:35.

Why God Made the Dog. Condensed from Moses Gaster: *Rumanian Bird and Beast Stories*, p. 79.

Why People Keep Dogs. This is a tale of the Yao people on Lake Nyasa in northern Mozambique, as told to Duff Macdonald. It is rewritten from his literal transcription as given in his *Africana, or the Heart of Heathen Africa,* vol. 2, pp. 333–334. Animal rescues man from cave is motif B549.4. It cites a Chinese tale as reference, to which this Yao tale can now be added.

Dog's Hoop. This story is based on the material in M. E. Opler: "Myths and Legends of the Lipan Apache Indians," *MAFS* 36: 203, 204.

How People Got the First Cat. This story is a composite of two versions of the cat-origin myth of the Ch'uan Miao people, an ethnic group living on the borders of Szechwan, Kweichow, and Yunnan provinces in western China. See D. C. Graham: "Songs and Stories of the Ch'uan Miao," *SMC* 123:1:1, 16.

Why Cat Eats First. This is a South Carolina Negro tale collected in Columbia, South Carolina, in 1914 and reported by Henry C. Davis: "Negro Folklore from South Carolina," *JAF* 27: 244–245. Why cat eats first (before washing) is motif A2545.2. A Lithuanian version, collected by Jonas Balys and published in 1940, is also referred to. There is also a European motif, especially popular in the Baltic countries: cat washes face before eating (K562) which belongs to the large and widespread group of folktales in which escape by subterfuge is the main idea. Dr. Stith Thompson reports five African borrowings of this anecdote in *The Folktale,* p. 289.

How the First Horse Was Made. This brief myth is told by the wild Kond tribes of northwestern Ganjam, in Orissa, India. See Verrier Elwin: *Tribal Myths of Orissa,* 384 #79. Creation of horse is motif A1881.

The Tinguians of northwestern Luzon, P. I., have a myth, collected by F.-C. Cole in 1907–1908, in which a certain man planted a rice field and fenced it. The rice grew and he began to notice that something was eating it up. So one night he went out to watch. After a while he heard the sound of wings and saw many beautiful creatures with wings come down into the rice. He caught one and cut off the wings and kept it. Soon it gave birth to a little foal. This is how horses came to earth but they do not fly anymore. You can see the scars on their legs, however, where the wings used to be. See F.-C. Cole: "Traditions of the Tinguian," *FMNHP* 180: 189 #64.

Why Goat Cannot Climb a Tree. This is a Haitian Creole folktale based on the literal version dictated to Alfred Métraux in the Gosseline Valley region of Haiti in 1948: edited by Robert A. Hall and published in his monograph, "Haitian Creole: Grammar, Texts, Vocabulary," *MAAA* 74: 146.

Why Sheep Does Not Come In out of the Rain. This is a North Carolina Negro anecdote, collected in Tulsa, Oklahoma, by B. A. Botkin from Anthony Dawson (aged 105), formerly a slave in North Carolina. See B. A. Botkin: *Lay My Burden Down,* pp. 14, 272.

Why Rabbit Has a Short Tail. This story is based on the tale as told to A. H. Fauset in 1925 by Daniel Mkato, a Baganda Negro from Uganda, East Africa, then a student at Tuskegee Institute in Alabama. It is published in Fauset's "Negro Tales from the South," *JAF* 40: 224 #13, under the title "Rabbit Counts Alligator's Family." Why rabbit (hare) has a short tail is motif A2378.4.1, citing European,

Japanese, Virginia Negro, and West Indian Negro references for it.

E. C. Parsons reported a folktale from Georgia in which once, when Rabbit went fishing, he had no bait; so he turned around and switched his tail in the water. A fish bit it off, so that is why Rabbit has a short tail. See E. C. Parsons: "Folklore from Georgia," *JAF* 47: 389. There is also an Indonesian version of the story in which mousedeer and crocodile play the rabbit and alligator roles.

How Bat Won the Ball Game. This story was popular among the Creek Indians of the southeastern United States and is based on the text given by John R. Swanton: "Myths and Tales of the Southeastern Indians," *BAEB* 88: 23. There is also a Cherokee Indian version.

Why Bat Flies Alone. This famous story as told here is based on the version collected by Jeremiah Curtin in 1884 among Modoc Indians then living in Lost River Valley, Oregon, and along the shores of Klamath and Tula Lakes. See his *Myths of the Modocs*, p. 213.

Motif B261.1 covers this story: bat in war of birds and quadrupeds joins first one side then the other and is discredited. The story occurs in most collections of Aesop's Fables and in general European folktale. There are versions from India and Japan, and from five African tribes.

Why Bear Sleeps All Winter. This is an old North Carolina Negro story based on the telling collected and published by W. W. Newell: "Animal Tales from North Carolina," *JAF* 11: 287–288.

How Chipmunk Got His Stripes. This famous origin myth of the Iroquois Indians is based on the version in Erminnie A. Smith: "Myths of the Iroquois," *BAER* 2: 80. The Thompson River Indians of British Columbia tell the same story and add that if Bear had caught and killed Chipmunk, mankind would have had to live in darkness forever instead of having alternate day and night, as we have today. See J. A. Teit: "Traditions of the Thompson River Indians of British Columbia," *MAFS* 6: 61–62 (1898).

How Chipmunk got his stripes is motif A2217.2. The myth stands equally, however, as a night-and-day origin myth and an animal-marking myth. Determination of night and day is motif A1172, citing this specific Iroquois tale and also Jewish, Indian, Maori, African, and South American Indian references. The concept of the creative power of song occurs frequently in this book. See Introduction, p. 10.

Why Lion Lives in the Forest. This Yao anecdote is based on the telling in Duff Macdonald: *Africana* 1: 293.

How Tiger Learned To Hunt. This is part of a story told to Dr. George M. Foster in 1940 by José Rodriguez, eighty-year-old Popoluca Indian of Soteapan in the mountains of southern Veracruz, Mexico. It is published in his monograph "Sierra Popoluca Folklore and Beliefs," *UCPAAE* 42: 225.

The tiger of this story is the little mountain ocelot of Mexico—called *tigre* everywhere in that country (*ibid.* p. 223*n*39).

149

How Whale Happens To Smoke a Pipe. This story of Kuloskap and Whale is condensed from J. D. Prince: "Passamaquoddy Texts," *PAES* 10: 27–31. For information about Kuloskap see notes to "How Loon Learned His Call," this book, p. 97.

Why Elephant and Whale Live Where They Do. This is a Bahama Negro story simplified from the dialect transcription made by Charles L. Edwards: "Bahama Songs and Stories," *MAFS* 3: 65 #2.

The first sentence reveals where the story came from. *Not in my time, not in your time, but in the old time* is the opening formula for the old tales which the old people remembered, either direct from Africa or from slaves who came to the Bahamas with Loyalist immigrants from the American colonies during the Revolution. Since neither elephants nor rabbits are native to the Bahamas, the story is certainly a relic of African tradition, where the elephant roamed and Hare or Little Hare was trickster, especially in Angola, Nigeria, and Dahomey. See M. J. Herskovits in *DFML* article "Rabbit," (2), 917d–918a. Br'er Rabbit of southern United States Negroes and B'Rabby in the Bahamas are both descendants of this same trickster.

Small animal challenges two large animals to tug-of-war; arranges that they unknowingly pull against each other is motif K22, with numerous African and New World Negro references.

Why Spider Has a Little Head and a Big Behind. This story is condensed from the Akan-Ashanti folktale as given in R. S. Rattray: *Akan-Ashanti Folktales*, pp. 67–71.

How Spider Got His Thread. This is a story of the Wishosk Indians around the shores of Humboldt Bay, northwestern California. They consisted of a few dozen people called Wishosk when Dr. Kroeber collected this story. They are now referred to as the Wiyot Indians, who numbered about one hundred individuals in 1910. This telling follows the myth as reported by A. L. Kroeber: "Wishosk Myths," *JAF* 18: 98.

Why spider has thread in back of body is motif A2356.2.8. There are Finnish and Estonian folktales (A2231.6) explaining that the spider once stole some thread from Christ and now has thread in the back of his body.

Why Porpoise Is Not a Fish. This is a myth of the Polynesian people of Mangaia, one of the Cook Islands, based on the recording, from native vernacular, of W. W. Gill: *Myths and Songs from the South Pacific*, p. 98.

Man transformed to porpoise is motif D127.6, citing tales from the Marquesas and from Tonga.

Malay peoples, too, have a tale ascribing human ancestry to the porpoise. Once an old wizard created all the fish in the sea. He went far out to sea in a boat, singing his magic spells and scattering mangrove leaves all over the waves. These turned into all kinds of fish: long and slender, short, round, flat, swimming and diving everywhere. When this was done the old fellow himself jumped in and was turned into a porpoise. See W. M. Skeat: *Malay Magic*, 308–309.

The two old tales seem singularly provocative today in the light of modern research with porpoises. The research is far from complete, but the dictum seems to be that the porpoise has an IQ as high, or higher, than man's, that he does communicate, and may eventually speak. Dr. John C. Lilly, director of the Communication Research

Institute in Miami, Florida, has been experimenting for years to find out if man and porpoise can learn to talk to each other—whether in English or porpoisese does not matter. One porpoise, named Elvar, surprised him one morning as they started their training session, by saying "All right, let's go." See R. L. Conly: "Porpoises: Our Friends in the Sea," *National Geographic Magazine* 130: 396–425 (Sept. 1966).

Why Dog Gnaws a Bone. This is a Tuscan proverb: #288 in *Proverbi Toscani,* a collection of Tuscan proverbs edited by Tullio Tentori and Jacopo Recupero, Grafica, Rome, 1959. (Contributed by Theresa C. Brakeley.)

Birds

Why the Birds Are Different Colors. This is a Negro story from the French Broad River region, North Carolina, based on the dialect recording of J. C. Branner: *How and Why Stories,* pp. 98–104.

Why Chicken Lives with Man. This is a story of the Mpongwe people of the West Coast of Africa, following the version given in H. R. Nassau: *Where Animals Talk: West African Folk Tales,* pp. 57–58. It is, of course, another one of the many, many tales in the world describing how some messenger from the animal or bird world is sent to get fire from man and becomes so contented with food, or warmth, or kindness in the new environment that he forgets his errand. See "Why the Animals Have No Fire," p. 57 (this book) and note, p. 147.

How Rooster Got His Comb. This is a story told by the Ch'uan Miao people of western China, based on the tale as reported by D. C. Graham: "Songs and Stories of the Ch'uan Miao," SMC 123 #1: 265. Other explanations of how cock (rooster) got his comb, comprising motif A2321.10, are given in tales from Lithuania and from Orissa, India.

Why Robin Has a Red Breast. This story is based on a folktale told by the people of the Lower Congo River, especially in the neighborhood of Sao Salvador in Angola, collected and published by John H. Weeks: *Congo Life and Folklore, Pt. 2: Thirty-Three Native Stories,* pp. 447–448.

The camwood powder mentioned is a fine red powder made by grinding together two pieces of wood from the camwood tree. It makes a bright red paste and was formerly used by the people of this region for personal decoration.

The robin is a loved and blessed bird in Christian legend because he plucked a thorn from the brow of Jesus on his way to Calvary. A drop of blood fell on his breast, which has been red ever since. This is motif A2221.2.2. There are Danish, Finnish, Livonian, Lithuanian, and Flemish versions of this tale, as well as Irish and English variants. Another explanation is that the robin carries water in his beak to souls suffering in hell, and the flames have tinged his breast. Something terrible, of course, will happen to anyone who kills a robin or tries to cage one.

Motif A2218.5—robin steals fire, has his breast scorched—comprises a saying of old people on the Island of Guernsey. There was no fire in Guernsey, they say, until one day a robin stole some and brought it to the island. His feathers got singed en route, however, and his breast has been red ever since.

How Kingfisher Got His Necklace. This is a story of the Chippewa Indians, collected by V. Barnouw from a seventy-year-old medicine priest on the Chippewa Reservation in northwestern Wisconsin in 1944. It comprises one brief episode of the long Wenebojo (Manabozho) cycle. See V. Barnouw: "A Psychological Interpretation of a Chippewa Origin Legend," *JAF* 68: 217.

The Chippewa and Ojibwa Indians are the same people and the terms are often used interchangeably. The Wisconsin groups, however, are often more specifically referred to as Chippewa.

The Wenebojo of this famous myth cycle plays the triple role of beneficent creator—culture hero—unpredictable trickster full of slyness, sadness, and anger. Wenebojo is the same character as Manabozho, Manabush, Messou, Michabo, Michabon, Nanabozho, Nanabush, Nenebojo, Nenebush, Wanibozhu, Wenebush, Winabojo. Among the Canadian Cree and Salteaux Indians, he is called Wissekedjack (often pronounced and written Whiskey Jack). Dr. Barnouw's informant used the form Wenebojo.

The kingfisher tale in the Salteaux version lacks the necklace episode but explains the crest. Origin of kingfisher's crest is motif A2321.5.

How Loon Learned His Call. This is a story of the Passamaquoddy Indians of Maine, based on the text as transcribed and published by John Dyneley Prince: "Passamaquoddy Texts," *PAES* 10: 25-27.

Kuloskap is the great, beneficent culture hero of the Indians of the Northeastern Woodlands. The Passamaquoddy Indians of Maine (of this story) call him Kuloskap. The Penobscot Indians (Maine) call him Kluskabe or Gluskabe. To the Malecites of New Brunswick and the Micmacs of Nova Scotia and New Brunswick, he is Gluskap (sometimes spelled Glooscap).

The Passamaquoddy say that Kuloskap, after giving mankind bows and arrows, hunting laws, and food, and happiness, was angry and grieved when he saw the people being greedy or cruel or unjust. He could not stay among them any more.

So he made one last great feast for all his creatures. All the animals and birds were there, and all the Indians came for this last farewell.

Then Kuloskap got into his canoe and went off singing. They could hear him singing long after the canoe was out of sight. Then when they turned to each other again, they were amazed to find that they could not speak to one another. Animals and men could no longer speak together and never will until Kuloskap returns.

The great white owl went into the deep woods and will not come out until Kuloskap comes back. The loons still call him, but he has not come back yet. See Prince: *PAES* 10: 49-55.

Owl. This is a medieval English moral tale from Gloucestershire, comprising motif A1958.0.1: owl is baker's daughter punished for stinginess. It is mentioned by Alexander H. Krappe: *The Science of Folklore,* p. 64, citing B. Thorpe: *Northern Mythology,* London, 1851, vol. 2, p. 25, Oskar Dähnhardt: *Natursagen* 2: 129f., and C. Swainson: *The Folk-Lore and Provincial Names of British Birds,* London, 1886, p. 123. Ophelia, in *Hamlet* (Act 4, Sc. 5, l. 41) bears witness to popular knowledge of the legend in Shakespeare's time when she says, "They say the owl was a baker's daughter."

152

Why Wagtail Wags Her Tail. This is a Rumanian folktale, based on the version from oral tradition given in Moses Gaster: *Rumanian Bird and Beast Stories,* p. 228.

The wagtail is a small singing bird of Europe and Asia (genus *Molacilla*): so named from the habit of jerking its tail up and down. The Irish say the wagtail has three drops of the Devil's blood on its tail and can't shake them off—but keeps trying. See *DFML,* 142d.

The aboriginal Ainu people in the northernmost islands of Japan have an ancient myth in which the creator sent Wagtail down to dry off the new slushy earth, which had just risen out of the primeval waters. The little wagtail fanned the world with his wings and beat and beat upon it with his tail until a few dry places were scattered around in the ocean. This was the Ainu's world: the islands the Ainu now occupy. And little Wagtail still bobs his tail up and down. See Leach: *The Beginning,* p. 205 and notes p. 207, citing J. Batchelor: *The Ainu and Their Folklore,* London, Religious Tract Society, 1901, pp. 582f.

Why Crow Has a Right to the First Corn. This story is part of the creation myth of the New York State Iroquois Indians, based on material given by Mrs. H. M. C. Converse: "Myths and Legends of the New York State Iroquois," *New York State Museum Bulletin* 125: 63–66, 185–186. See also *DFML,* 307c, 430a, 474b. The Narraganset Indians (an Algonquian tribe) tell much the same story: one day a crow came to them from the southwest bearing a kernel of corn in one ear and a bean in the other. Henceforth crows were never driven out of their cornfields because they "had the first right." See E. and J. Lehrer: *Folklore and Odysseys of Food and Medicinal Plants,* Tudor Publishing Company, New York, 1962, p. 19 (reference supplied by Marion D. Robertson). See also *ERE* 1: 510b. The Portuguese, too, have a proverb: *O primeiro milho é dos pardais*—The earliest corn belongs to the sparrow. See George Monteiro: "Proverbs and Proverbial Phrases of the Continental Portuguese," *Western Folklore* 22: 35 (1963).

How Crane Got His Long Beak. This brief myth is told by the Gumaitj linguistic group of the Jiritja moiety of the Murngin people of Arnhemland, Australia. As told here, the tale is based on the version given in Elkin and Berndt: *Art in Arnhem Land,* 45–46.

Insects, Reptiles, and Fish

Why the Flea Jumps. This is a Tuscan proverb, #332 in *Proverbi Toscani,* a collection of Tuscan proverbs edited by Tullio Tentori and Jacopo Recupero, Grafica, Rome, 1959. (Contributed by Theresa C. Brakeley.)

Why Ants Live Everywhere. This is a Burmese folktale following the version as given in E. D. Edwards: *Bamboo, Lotus, and Palm,* p. 252, citing Sir J. G. Scott (Shuay Yoe): *The Burman, His Life and Notions,* 2 vols., Macmillan Company, London, 1882.

Why Ants Carry Large Bundles. This is an Ashanti story of the old Gold Coast Colony, collected from students at the Training Institution for Teachers at Accra, and greatly condensed from the version given in Barker and Sinclair: *West African Folk-Tales,* pp. 66–69. Spider hands box to ant and won't take it back is motif A2243.1.

Why Fly Rubs His Hands Together. This story is a fragment of the long creation myth of the Luiseño Indians of the coast of southern California. See C. G. Du Bois: "Mythology of the Mission Indians: #1 San Luiseño Creation Myth," *JAF* 19: 60.
     For a description of a fire drill, see "Creator Makes—," p. 41.

Why Grasshopper Spits Tobacco Juice. This is a Penobscot Indian story, one of the collection made by Dr. Frank G. Speck over the summer months of 1909–1916 from the Penobscot Indians in the Penobscot River valley of north central Maine. See F. G. Speck: "Penobscot Tales and Religious Beliefs," *JAF* 48: 41–42 #13. For explanation of Gluskabe, see "How Loon Learned His Call," p. 97 and note, p. 152.

Why Crocodile Does Not Eat Hen. This is a tale told by the Fjort Negroes, a Bantu people of the old French Congo, specifically of the two provinces north of the Congo or Zaire River. It follows the tale as given by R. E. Dennett: *Notes on the Folklore of the Fjort,* 106–107. It is classified as a legal story, one revealing the moral code of the Fjorts and their concepts of right and wrong. It is one of many such tales cited during the administration of justice to prove a point or to establish a precedent. When told under such circumstances, it often ends with the words ". . . and the people said it was right." See also Dennett: pp. ix, xi.

How Rattlesnake Got His Fangs. This story is part of the long creation myth of the Luiseño Indians of coastal southwestern California. As here told it is based on the recording of Dr. Constance G. Du Bois: "Mythology of the Mission Indians: #1 San Luiseño Creation Myth," *JAF* 19: 54. The Luiseño Indians took their name from the old Mission San Luis Rey de Francia. In 1925 these people numbered fewer than five hundred.

How Tadpoles Lost Their Tails. This is a Negro story from the region of the French Broad River, North Carolina, based on the dialect recording of John C. Branner: *How and Why Stories,* pp. 31–35.

Why Frogs Croak in Wet Weather. This is a Korean story collected in Seoul by Professor Zong in-Sob in 1944 and published as story #18 in his *Folk Tales from Korea,* pp. 34–35. Why frogs croak in wet weather is motif A2426.4.1.2, which cites only the Korean reference.

How Turtle Keeps from Getting Wet. This is a story of the Natchez Indians formerly living in the southern Mississippi Valley. It was collected by John R. Swanton between the years 1908–1914 near Braggs, Oklahoma, from a man named Watt Sam, one of the few living speakers of the old Natchez language at that time. He, however, told Dr. Swanton that he had heard the tale from a Creek Indian. See John R. Swanton: "Myths and Tales of the Southeastern Indians," *BAEB* 88: 1, 254 #28.

Why Flounder's Two Eyes Are on the Same Side of His Face. This is a folktale collected by Dr. S. H. Elbert in 1947 on the island of Kapingamarangi in the Pacific.

Kapingamarangi lies about four hundred miles south of Truk in the Carolines (Micronesia), but it is an island of Polynesian people and culture. See S. H. Elbert: "Uta-Matua and Other Tales of Kapingamarangi," *JAF* 62: 245.

Why Jellyfish Has No Shell. This story is a composite of the tale as elaborated by B. H. Chamberlain in "The Silly Jelly-Fish," #13 of the old *Japanese Fairy Tale Series,* and as given by Keigo Seki: *Folktales of Japan,* "The Monkey's Liver," pp. 25–27. In Keigo Seki's version from Kikai Island, however, it is a dog who is sent ashore to bring the monkey to Neinya and the octopus and swellfish who were beaten for tattling the secret. Dr. Seki reports the tale as included in the eleventh-century Japanese compilation *Konjaku Monogatari* and in the Buddhist *Jataka,* vol. 2, 110–112.

The tale in all versions bears witness to belief in the separable soul: i.e., belief that the soul (heart, liver, life) can exist apart from the living body of its owner, in some plant, bird, animal, egg, or inanimate object. Monkey caught for heart (liver) makes captor believe he has left it at home is motif K544, citing European, Indian, Jewish, Philippine, Zanzibar, and Japanese references.

Why Crab's Eyes Stick Out. This story is based on and condensed from the tale in R. E. Dennett: *Notes on the Folklore of the Fjort,* 123–124. Why crab's eyes stick out from his body is motif A2231.10. See also *DFML,* 832a: crab's eyes popped up out of his body when he beat the god's forbidden drum.

Plants

Why Some Trees Are Evergreen. This is a Cherokee Indian myth based on the presentation given by James Mooney: "Myths of the Cherokee Indians," *BAER* 19, Pt. 1: 240.

How the Coconut Tree Was Saved. This is a folktale of the mountain Apayao people of northwestern Luzon, P. I., based on the literal version given by L. L. Wilson: *Apayao Life and Legends,* p. 97.

How Bean Got His Stripe. This story comprises the final episodes of a famous European folktale, most typically represented in *Grimm's Fairy Tales,* #18, usually entitled "The Bean, the Straw, and the Coal."

These episodes are specified in four separate motifs. Why Bean has black stripe is motif A2793.1. Bean laughs till it splits: cause of black stripe is motif A2741.1, citing Estonian, Danish, Flemish, and Livonian references. There are also two New World analogs: one Ojibwa Indian and one Jamaica Negro. Bean, straw, and coal go journeying is motif F1025.1, citing German references and one from the Lepchas of the Himalaya mountains. Skillful tailor sews bean together after bean has split from laughing is motif F662.3, citing only the Grimm tale #18. Stith Thompson reports (see *The Folktale,* 223) that old European sixteenth-century fable collections often included this tale.

Cherokee Indian mothers often take beans which have split open in cooking and rub them on the lips of their children. The laughing bean makes smiling children, they say. See J. Mooney: "Myths of the Cherokee Indians," *BAEB* 19, Pt. 1: 424.

How Yams Got Their Eyes. This story is a composite of the Easter Island myth, as deciphered from the strange hieroglyphic script of the famous and baffling wooden tablets of Easter Island by Werner Wolff: *Island of Death,* pp. 92–96, plus the versions given by Alfred Métraux: "Ethnology of Easter Island," *BPBMB* 160: 374 and by J. M. Brown: *The Riddle of the Pacific,* London, 1927, p. 181: both cited by Wolff, pp. 97, 98. The hat of the red flying bird is, of course, its crest. The origin of yams is motif A1423.1, citing references for Samoa, Tonga, New Zealand, New Guinea, and Easter Island.

Constellations

The Great Bear. This is the famous North American Indian bear-hunt story known and told from Alaska to the Pueblos, but especially a favorite of Central and Northeastern Woodlands Algonquian tribes. All tribes feature specific variations, but the bear fleeing across the sky followed by seven, or three, hunters is the basic explanation.

This Micmac Indian version from Nova Scotia is condensed from S. Hagar: "The Celestial Bear," *JAF* 13: 92–103. Scholars believe it to be completely indigenous. The French Recollect missionary explorer Chrétien Leclerq gives the earliest reference to it in his *Nouvelle relation de la Gaspésie,* Paris, 1691.

The saw-whet of the story is the tiny Acadian owl. The moosebird is the famous Canada jay. Origin of Great Bear is motif A771. For a synopsis of the Iroquois version, see *DFML,* 464cd.

This beautiful and conspicuous constellation has fascinated mankind in every part of the world where it is visible; and almost everywhere it has been called a bear, from the ancient Hebrew Dōbh (Bear) and the classic Greek Callisto to the Koryaks in Siberia, who call it Notakavya, the One Who Walks Around the Earth. See *DFML,* 1152a.

Why People Watch the Dipper. This is a myth told by the Tahltan Indians of the North Pacific Coast, based on the version given by James A. Teit: "Tahltan Tales," *JAF* 32: 228.

Pleiades. This is a Cherokee Indian story condensed from the presentation given in James Mooney: "Myths of the Cherokee Indians," *BAER* 19, Pt. 1: 258–259. See also *DFML,* articles "Dancers," 296bc; "Pleiades," 874d–875c.

The *gatayusti,* or wheel-and-stick game, of the story is a very ancient game and was widespread among Indians of the southern United States. They used a stone wheel about two inches thick at the edge and two spans round. The poles were about eight feet long, smooth and tapered at each end. The players began the game abreast of each other, six yards from the end of the playground. One hurled the stone wheel, on edge, in as straight a line as possible toward the other end of the playground. The boys would then run and each would dart his pole, as near as he could guess to the speed of the wheel, so that the end of it might lie close to the wheel. The player whose pole came nearest the oftenest won the game. See Mooney: *BAER* 19, Pt. 1: 434.

Escape to the stars: fugitives rise in air and become stars is motif R321, citing Greek, Hindu, Japanese, Korean, Eskimo, and North American and South American Indian references.

156

Udleqdjun in the Sky. This is a tale from the Eskimos around Cumberland Sound, Baffin Island, collected by Dr. Franz Boas during the years 1883–1884, and given in his famous report: "The Central Eskimo," *BAER* 6: 636–637.

Bibliography

W. H. Barker and C. Sinclair: *West African Folk-Tales,* George G. Harrap & Co., Ltd., London, 1917

Victor Barnouw: A Psychological Interpretation of a Chippewa Origin Legend, *JAF* 68: 73–85, 211–223, 341–355 (1955)

R. and C. Berndt. *See* Elkin

Franz Boas: The Central Eskimo, *BAER* 6:401–669 (1888)

Waldemar Bogoras: Chukchee Tales, *JAF* 41:297–452 (1928)

Benjamin A. Botkin: *Lay My Burden Down,* The University of Chicago Press, Chicago, 1954

Theresa C. Brakeley: personal communications

John C. Branner: *How and Why Stories,* Henry Holt & Company, Inc., New York, 1921

Henry Callaway: *Nursery Tales, Traditions, and Histories of the Zulus,* Trübner and Company, London, 1868

B. H. Chamberlain: The Silly Jelly-Fish, #13 of *Japanese Fairy Tale Series,* 16 nos., Kobunsha, Tokyo, n. d.; c. 1888–1890

Fay-Cooper Cole: Traditions of the Tinguian, *FMNHP* 180 (1915)

Mrs. H. M. C. Converse: Myths and Legends of the New York State Iroquois, *New York State Museum Bulletin* 125 (1908)

Jeremiah Curtin: *Myths of the Modocs,* Little, Brown & Company, Boston, 1912

Henry C. Davis: Negro Folklore from South Carolina, *JAF* 27:241–254 (1914)

Elphinstone Dayrell: *Folk Stories from Southern Nigeria,* Longmans, Green & Company, London, 1910

R. E. Dennett: *Notes on the Folklore of the Fjort* (French Congo), David Nutt, London, 1898

Constance G. Du Bois: Mythology of the Mission Indians: #1 San Luiseño Creation Myth, *JAF* 19:52–60 (1906)

Charles L. Edwards: Bahama Songs and Stories, *MAFS* 3 (1895)

E. D. Edwards: *Bamboo, Lotus, and Palm,* William Hodge and Company, Ltd., London, Edinburgh, Glasgow, 1918

Samuel H. Elbert: Uta-Matua and Other Tales of Kapingamaringi, *JAF* 62:240–246 (1949)

A. P. Elkin and R. and C. Berndt: *Art in Arnhem Land,* The University of Chicago Press, Chicago, 1950

Verrier Elwin: *Tribal Myths of Orissa,* Oxford University Press, London, 1954

————: *Myths of the North-East Frontier of India,* North-East Frontier Agency, Shillung, 1958

157

E. N. Fallaize: article **sun, moon, and stars,** *ERE* xii:48a–103b
Arthur Huff Fauset: Negro Tales from the South, *JAF* 40:213–303 (1927)
George M. Foster: Sierra Popoluca Folklore and Beliefs, *UCPAAE* 42:177–250 (1945)
Douglas C. Fox. *See* Frobenius
Jerome Fried. *See* Leach
Leo Frobenius and Douglas C. Fox: *African Genesis,* Stackpole Sons, New York, 1937

Moses Gaster: *Rumanian Bird and Beast Stories,* Folk-Lore Society, London, 1915
Albert S. Gatchet: Popular Rimes from Mexico, *JAF* 2:48–53 (1889)
William Wyatt Gill: *Myths and Songs from the South Pacific,* Henry S. King and
    Company, London, 1876
David Crockett Graham: Songs and Stories of the Ch'uan Miao, *SMC* 123 #1:1–355
    (1954)
Grimm's Fairy Tales, Pantheon Books, Inc., New York, 1944

Stansbury Hagar: The Celestial Bear, *JAF* 13:92–103 (1900)
Robert A. Hall: Haitian Creole: Grammer, Texts, Vocabulary, *MAAA* 74 (1953)
James Hastings, ed.: *Encyclopedia of Religion and Ethics,* 13 vols., Charles Scribner's
    Sons, New York, 1908–1927
Uno Holmberg: Siberian Mythology, *MAR* 4, Boston, 1927

Alexander H. Krappe: *The Science of Folklore,* W. W. Norton & Company, Inc., New
    York, 1964: reprint of 1930 ed.
A. L. Kroeber: Wishosk Myths, *JAF* 18:85–107 (1905)
————: Handbook of the Indians of California, *BAEB* 78 (1925)

Maria Leach: *The Beginning: Creation Myths Around the World,* Funk & Wagnalls
    Company, New York, 1956
————: *God Had a Dog: Folklore of the Dog,* Rutgers University Press, New Bruns-
    wick, 1961
———— and Jerome Fried: *Standard Dictionary of Folklore, Mythology, and Legend,*
    2 vols., Funk & Wagnalls Company, New York, 1949–1950

Duff Macdonald: *Africana, or the Heart of Heathen Africa,* 2 vols., Simpkin, Mar-
    shall, Ltd., London, 1882
Alfred Métraux: Myths of the Toba and Pilagá Indians of the Gran Chaco, *MAFS*
    40 (1946)
————: Ethnography of the Chaco, *BAEB* 143:1:197–370 (1946)
————: Ethnology of Easter Island, *BPBMB* 160 (1940)
James Mooney: Myths of the Cherokee Indians, *BAER* 19, Pt. 1:3–548 (1897–1898)
George P. Murdock: *Africa: Its Peoples and Their Culture History,* McGraw-Hill
    Book Company, Inc., New York, 1959

H. R. Nassau: *Where Animals Talk: West African Folk Tales,* Goreham Press,
    Boston, 1912
W. W. Newell: Animal Tales from North Carolina, *JAF* 11:284–292 (1898)

M. E. Opler: Myths and Tales of the Jicarilla Apache Indians, *MAFS* 31 (1938)
———: Myths and Legends of the Lipan Apache Indians, *MAFS* 36 (1940)

K. Langloh Parker: *Australian Legendary Tales,* The Viking Press, Inc., New York, 1966
John Dyneley Prince: Passamaquoddy Texts, *PAES* 10 (1921)

Knud Rasmussen: *Eskimo Folk-Tales,* Gyldendal, London, Copenhagen, Christiania, 1921
R. S. Rattray: *Akan-Ashanti Folktales,* Clarendon Press, Oxford, 1930
Gladys Reichard: An Analysis of Coeur d'Alene Myths, *MAFS* 41 (1947)

Keigo Seki: *Folktales of Japan,* The University of Chicago Press, Chicago, 1963
C. Sinclair. *See* Barker
Walter M. Skeat: *Malay Magic: Introduction to the Folklore and Popular Religion of the Malay Peninsula,* Macmillan & Co., Ltd., London and New York, 1900
Erminnie A. Smith: Myths of the Iroquois, *BAER* 2:47–111 (1883)
Frank G. Speck: *Catawba Texts,* Columbia University Press, New York, 1934
———: Penobscot Tales and Religious Beliefs, *JAF* 48:1–107 (1935)
Julian H. Steward, ed.: Handbook of South American Indians, *BAEB* 143, 6 vols., 1946–1950; vol. 7, 1960
Snorri Sturluson: *Prose Edda,* tr. A. G. Brodeur, American-Scandinavian Foundation, Oxford University Press, New York, 1929
John R. Swanton: Myths and Tales of the Southeastern Indians, *BAEB* 88 (1929)

James A. Teit: Traditions of the Lillooet Indians of British Columbia, *JAF* 25:287–381 (1912)
———: Tahltan Tales, *JAF* 32:198–252 (1919)
Tullio Tentori and Jacopo Recupero: *Proverbi Toscani,* Grafica, Rome, 1959
Stith Thompson: *Motif Index of Folk Literature,* 2d. ed., 6 vols., Indiana University Press, Bloomington, 1955–1958
———: *The Folktale,* Dryden Press, New York, 1946
——— and Jonas Balys: *Oral Tales of India,* Indiana University Press, Bloomington, 1958

John H. Weeks: *Congo Life and Folklore, Pt. 2: Thirty-Three Native Stories,* Religious Tract Society, London, 1911
Laurence L. Wilson: *Apayao Life and Legends,* Southeast Asia Institute, 1947
Werner Wolff: *Island of Death: A New Key to Easter Island's Culture,* J. J. Augustin, New York, 1948

Zong in-Sob: *Folk Tales from Korea,* Routledge and Kegan Paul, London, 1952

MARIA LEACH is one of America's best-known folklorists and the author of many books for children and adults. She is the compiler-editor of the distinguished two-volume *Standard Dictionary of Folklore, Mythology, and Legend* and other outstanding folklore collections for children and for adults, including *God Had a Dog: Folklore of the Dog*. Mrs. Leach is a member of the American Folklore Society, of which she has been a Councilor, of the American Anthropological Association, the American Dialect Society, the Northeast Folklore Society, the Canadian Folksong Society, the International Folk Music Council, and the American Indian Ethnohistoric Conference. Maria Leach lives in Nova Scotia.